The Resilient Product Manager

Getting through uncertainty, prioritization, and delivering business results under pressure

Kaelin Rhun

Published by: GitforGits

Publisher: Sonal Dhandre

www.gitforgits.com

Printed in India

First Printing: March 2025

ISBN: 978-93-49174-84-9

Cover Design by: Kitten Publishing

Disclaimer:

This book, including all its text, diagrams, and illustrations, is an original work developed for educational and informational purposes. The content is not affiliated with, endorsed by, or sponsored by any other company, brand, or entity referenced within. Every effort has been made to ensure that no copyrighted or trademarked material has been copied or misused in this book. All diagrams and illustrations are created by the professionals of GitforGits using Canva platform with royalty-free assets.

If you believe that any content in this book infringes upon your copyright or trademark, please contact us immediately at support@gitforgits.com. Upon notification, corrective action will be taken promptly.

Prologue

Managing products isn't for the faint of heart. It's all about being able to deal with uncertainty, make big decisions even when you don't have all the info, and get different teams on the same page, especially when the market, the tech, and what customers want is always changing. Over the years, I've been lucky enough to learn from my own experiences, as well as from the smart insights of my colleagues, mentors, and some of the most creative product minds I know. This book is the result of all that learning—it's a collection of seven different real-world examples that have been boiled down into useful advice.

We chose each case study for a reason. Some show how metrics can be like the north star that keeps a team on track and honest. Some people explain how data sampling, confidence intervals, and scenario modeling can break down massive, complex datasets into something that can be used to make decisions. A few of them show how important it is to have a plan for working together, like keeping the same pace, setting up checkpoints for decisions, and using shared documents. This helps keep things moving without losing clarity. There are stories of how teams have dealt with things like operational crises, spikes in cancellations, or unexpected user behavior, and turned those challenges into opportunities for innovation.

What you'll read here isn't just some theoretical stuff. These are real-life examples of product teams adapting under pressure. They're creating playbooks for metric prioritization, engineering scalable experiments, running workshops that identify the true root causes, and implementing systems that make performance transparent. As a product leader, you'll get to see the human side of things: the negotiations, the creative problem-solving, the constant questioning of assumptions, and the small process refinements that lead to huge results. The strength of these stories is in their variety. It's all about optimizing customer engagement and stabilizing service performance, and the principles of product management stay the same: listen closely to the data and the people, break down the complexity into solvable parts, prioritize relentlessly, and keep the customer at the center of every decision.

This book isn't going to hand you a magic formula for success. Instead, it's meant to give you patterns—mental models and tactical approaches you can adapt to your own context. Whether you're a seasoned product manager or just starting out, these lessons will help you build the resilience, clarity, and adaptability that define the very best in this craft.

Content

Preface

After chatting with other product managers, talking with industry pros, and getting insights from all sorts of real-world situations, this book puts together patterns and practices that have worked well when the pressure's on. The seven case stories in this book show how these companies dealt with situations that the usual approach didn't cover. Whether it was rethinking how to predict engagement, estimating demand in uncertain conditions, or containing operational breakdowns before they spiraled, the people behind these stories had to adapt quickly, think clearly, and act with purpose.

You'll learn how to take raw data and turn it into useful information. You'll learn about things like sampling strategies, confidence intervals, and sensitivity testing. You'll see how teams align on priorities through collaborative workshops, root-cause analysis, and impact-effort scoring. You'll learn how proofs-of-concept and guardrails help you to confidently expand your business, and how well-designed dashboards can provide early warnings so you can avoid any issues before they impact your customers. We use the HEART framework to align our product goals, fishbone diagrams to cut through complexity, prioritization scorecards to focus our energy where it matters, and monitoring setups to keep the team ahead of the curve.

While the contexts vary, the lessons are universal. This book is for product managers who know that resilience isn't about avoiding problems—it's about being ready to handle them no matter where they come from. It's a shared strategy guide for those who want to lead with clarity when it matters most.

In this book you will learn to:

- Translate complex data into clear insights that directly guide strategic product decisions under uncertainty.
- Build alignment through collaborative frameworks that unite product, engineering, and business teams on priorities.
- Apply sampling and estimation methods to make confident decisions even with incomplete or noisy datasets.
- Use structured prioritization techniques to maximize ROI while balancing speed, impact, and resource constraints.
- Implement early-warning dashboards that detect anomalies before customers experience a drop in service.
- Conduct root-cause analysis to uncover hidden issues that metrics alone may fail to reveal.
- Create lightweight proofs-of-concept to validate assumptions before committing resources to full-scale initiatives.

- Document and share decisions, assumptions, and learnings to maintain clarity across fast-moving teams.
- Blend operational and financial indicators to ensure product success is tied to tangible business outcomes.
- Develop resilience by anticipating failure modes and preparing mitigation tactics that can be deployed quickly.

GitforGits

Prerequisites

Ideally, you'll have a solid understanding of product management concepts, be comfortable with interpreting simple metrics, and have some experience working with teams across different functions. If you're curious about solving problems under constraints and you're open to learning from real-world case studies, you'll get a lot out of this book.

Codes Usage

Are you in need of some helpful code examples to assist you in your programming and documentation? Look no further! Our book offers a wealth of supplemental material, including code examples and exercises.

Not only is this book here to aid you in getting your job done, but you have our permission to use the example code in your programs and documentation. However, please note that if you are reproducing a significant portion of the code, we do require you to contact us for permission.

But don't worry, using several chunks of code from this book in your program or answering a question by citing our book and quoting example code does not require permission. But if you do choose to give credit, an attribution typically includes the title, author, publisher, and ISBN. For example, "The Resilient Product Manager by Kaelin Rhun".

If you are unsure whether your intended use of the code examples falls under fair use or the permissions outlined above, please do not hesitate to reach out to us at support@gitforgits.com.

We are happy to assist and clarify any concerns.

Acknowledgement

I owe a tremendous debt of gratitude to GitforGits, for their unflagging enthusiasm and wise counsel throughout the entire process of writing this book. Their knowledge and careful editing helped make sure the piece was useful for people of all reading levels and comprehension skills. In addition, I'd like to thank everyone involved in the publishing process for their efforts in making this book a reality. Their efforts, from copyediting to advertising, made the project what it is today.

Finally, I'd like to express my gratitude to everyone who has shown me unconditional love and encouragement throughout my life. Their support was crucial to the completion of this book. I appreciate your help with this endeavour and your continued interest in my career.

Acknowledgement

CRAFTING A GADGET-SHARING MARKETPLACE

India's cities and villages have seen the growth of digital marketplaces very quickly, changing the way people buy and sell things and services without the need for traditional middlemen. As internet speeds get faster and cheaper, entrepreneurs and regular people alike create platforms that connect supply and demand. Well-known brands like Amazon and Flipkart rule the retail market, while a new generation of niche startups lets people rent power tools, designer clothes, and even luxury cars. At the same time, peer-to-peer sharing sites are growing to meet the needs of people who want access to ownership in Asia, Europe, and the Americas. Because people are price aware and want to get the most out of their assets, these marketplaces use trust-building tools like reviews, identity checks, and escrow payments to get around long-standing problems.

On the other hand, mobile-first designs and built-in digital wallets make it easier to send and receive money. The rise of these kinds of services marks the start of a sharing economy that is powered by data, connectivity, and community-driven validation. In this economy, anyone with an idle asset can find a global stage to make money, and renters can afford to use equipment that might otherwise sit empty. The GadgetShare grows out of this rich ground to become a case study in how to fix fragmentation.

User Demands and Market Opportunities

Persona Development

The founders would spend late nights scrolling through local Facebook groups, WhatsApp communities, and online forums, as if they were treasure hunters looking for a chest buried somewhere. One of them, an amateur filmmaker named Ravi, started the habit when he said he wanted to hold a back-yard showing without a reliable 4K projector. As a reaction, postings showed hopeful glimpses of a fragmented network: one person was selling a DSLR for half the price of an agency, and another was advertising a portable projector that had only been used for movie nights in suburban gardens on the weekends. The random messages had the allure of a secret society, but each one threatened to end in failure when expiration dates came up out of the blue, hidden fees showed up like unwanted guests, and payment options shrunk to time-consuming bank transfers. As neighborly excitement turned into a never-ending stream of unanswered questions, they could feel their anger rising. It gave the founders an electric moment of clarity during which they came up with the idea for GadgetShare, a peer-to-peer platform that would bring together all the random talk into an easy-to-use marketplace with accurate listings, clear terms, and smooth transactions.

Once the team made detailed personas that showed the wide range of possible users, a clear mission began to take shape. First, they talked to Anjali, a college student in a rural town who was eager to go to photography workshops with borrowed DSLRs but had trouble getting them because deliveries were often scheduled for days after they were supposed to come. A big difference became clear when I talked to Rohit, the founder of an urban company who almost went crazy when important microphones went missing minutes before a live product demo. As they listened to Maya, a community leader, talk about how hard it is to share a single projector between several local schools on a tight budget, they felt a wave of empathy. It was clear that even weekend influencers like Sam, who is known for having pop-up movie theaters, got tired of searching through random posts to find rentable gear. Each persona was broken down into three main ideas: proximity, trust, and clear pricing. These ideas were then used to create story sketches that showed different people's motives and pain points. The GadgetShare wanted to make an experience that feels as personal as an offer from a neighbor and as reliable as a rental service that has been around for a long time.

Survey Insights

To validate their assumptions and refine these personas, the founders distributed detailed surveys at co-working hubs, rural training centers and college campuses. They gathered more than 500 responses, asking about gadget usage frequency, sharing willingness, preferred booking windows and top trust factors. In follow-up interviews, participants recalled hidden charges, cleaning fees, late penalties and tax surcharges, and unpredictable pick-up schedules. Many renters expressed anxiety over collateral deposits, while owners feared device damage or theft. That feedback highlighted the need for peer reviews, secure deposit handling and flexible logistics options. It also underscored demand for intuitive mobile interfaces with clear status updates and notifications at every step.

The survey findings merged with regional rental data, revealed nuanced demand clusters. Heat maps pinpointed urban neighborhoods, particularly creative districts, where cameras could circulate within hours. Rural clusters emerged around agricultural colleges and community halls, where projectors were in demand during weekday seminars. Weekend spikes among independent filmmakers suggested brief, high-intensity rental windows. Layering weather and event calendars exposed seasonal trends: outdoor event organizers sought projectors in monsoon season for indoor screenings, while amateur photographers booked drones during clear autumn weekends. These insights led to a targeted pilot in two city districts and three villages, allowing the team to test delivery routes, insurance workflows and customer-support scripts before a broader roll-out.

Rough but Strong Vision

We put together some stories and numbers, and we were able to identify five main problems: not knowing the state of the device, hidden costs, the chance of returns being late, complicated logistics, and the lack of trust mechanisms. Putting all these problems together into one statement:

"Let's make it so people can share gadgets safely and easily across different communities"

And, this created a clear goal that guided decisions about the product's design, development goals, and user experience. So, the team came up with a solid product vision that hits the current needs and gets the creative juices flowing for future innovations. They were:

- If we had a real-time access calendar that could adjust to different time zones, there would be no double bookings.

- An in-app escrow system that works with common payment methods would protect deposits and give owners their money back right away when returns are successful.
- It had a reputation engine with peer reviews, photos of the gadget's condition, and verification badges to build trust in the community.
- There were a bunch of options for getting things delivered, like picking up from a friend's place based on where you are, getting something delivered by a courier whenever you want, and having a partner drop it off.

Later on, the features that people are looking for will make them want to keep using it. There are some benefits for loyalty that are like games, like share-streak badges and referral bonuses, that would get people to use the service again and help the community. You'd be able to get your car serviced more easily and worry less if you make deals with nearby auto repair shops and insurance companies. We could have pop-up test days and interactive community events to show off the new gadgets and get real-time feedback. Finally, it'll show how the platform is being used, suggest the best prices, and predict demand. That'll give platform owners and strategic planners more influence.

Technical Landscape and Legacy Constraints

System Architecture Challenges

When the GadgetShare team first examined their prototype's infrastructure, they found two aging on-premises servers running a monolithic Linux application. That single codebase handled user authentication, gadget catalog management, booking workflows and notifications, all tied to one default MySQL database. Without sharding or replication, query performance slowed as data grew, and unrotated logs filled disk space. Deployment relied on manual scripts that built WAR files and ran remote SSH commands, while security overlooked expired SSL certificates and outdated password hashing.

These findings revealed five critical challenges:

1. **Monolithic API Boundaries**

   A single runtime hosted every endpoint, device search, booking creation, payment processing. Any logic change forced a full rebuild and redeploy of the entire application, extending release cycles and risking downtime.

2. **Database Performance Bottlenecks**

   One MySQL server managed all reads and writes. Lock contention and slow JOIN queries degraded user experience, and lack of proper indexes allowed response times to grow exponentially.

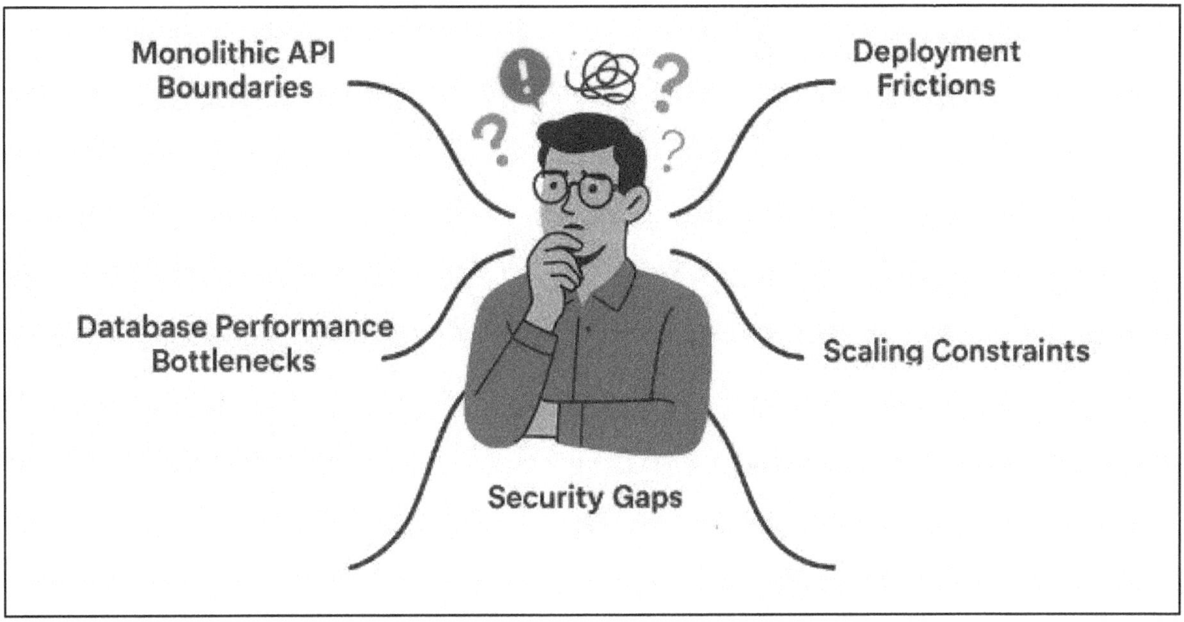

Fig 1.1 System Architecture Challenges

3. **Deployment Frictions**

Releases depended on ad-hoc shell scripts and a single DevOps engineer. Configuration drift between staging and production led to frequent environment mismatches, and no automated rollback meant extended outages during failures.

4. **Security Gaps**

Credentials were hashed with weak algorithms and stored in unencrypted backups. The API lacked rate limiting, and SSL certificates expired without warning, exposing data to brute-force and man-in-the-middle risks.

5. **Scaling Constraints**

Vertical scaling hit limits as CPU and memory spikes during peak traffic forced manual throttling. Without containerization or horizontal scaling, the team could not respond quickly to sudden demand shifts.

Strengthening Foundation (Weeks 1-4)

The team split their large, single codebase into smaller, independent services. The authentication, catalog management, and booking each have their own repository with clear version tags so that updates can happen without rebuilding everything. They speed up the database by adding indexes on slow queries and creating a read-only replica for reporting work, which keeps the main database quick for users. We switched from using manual scripts to an automated pipeline using GitLab CI for deployment. Every time you push a code update, the tests run, the Docker images are built, and the new version is released with blue/green deployments, you'll see that downtime disappears and rollbacks are just one command away. They made things more secure by switching to bcrypt password hashing, using OAuth 2.0 tokens, and putting an API gateway in front of all services to put limits on the rate, block IP addresses, and automatically renew SSL certificates.

Scaling for Growth (Weeks 5–10)

As usage went up, each service became a Docker container managed by Kubernetes. This containerization made it so that the system could automatically scale based on real-time load. The team moved noncritical tasks, like email notifications and billing updates, to RabbitMQ queues. This way, workers could process these asynchronously and keep the main API fast.

The database tables were moved to regional shards, and ProxySQL is in charge of directing queries to the right shard. That partitioning reduced contention and improved response times for users across different locations. And the observability improved with Prometheus metrics and Grafana dashboards. When there were high error rates or CPU spikes, we sent alerts to Slack to make sure we could find the problem and fix it quickly.

Future-Proofing (Weeks 11+)

Imagine facing a sudden surge in user requests for gadget photos and videos, with no extra servers ready to pick up the slack. What if a single function could spring into action whenever it's needed, then vanish without a trace when demand subsides? By moving image thumbnail creation into AWS Lambda, the team achieved just that: each upload triggers a lightweight function that generates every required size, then shuts itself down. No pre-provisioned instances sit idle during quiet periods. Billing reflects only actual usage, so costs grow in step with demand and never spike unnecessarily. Meanwhile, every code change flows through an automated pipeline where SonarQube analyzes code quality and vulnerability tests probe for security gaps. Reports arrive alongside build logs, offering an audit trail that proves adherence to strict data-privacy regulations. Whenever a new vulnerability surfaces, the pipeline flags it immediately, preventing risky code from reaching production.

What happens when a key service suddenly fails or a network link slows to a crawl? To find out, testers regularly inject faults into staging environments: they disable mock databases, throttle API responses and shutter individual service instances. Circuit breakers trip, redirecting traffic to backup routes or cached responses so that end users experience only minimal delays. Detailed dashboards show fallback paths kicking in, then recovering gracefully once normal operations return. The team gathers actionable insights about system behavior under stress with the help of running these drills on a schedule that mimics peak traffic patterns. Throughout this exercise, evidence accumulates that modular codebases, finely tuned databases, automated delivery pipelines and serverless functions form the backbone of a resilient, high-performance platform. Each experiment reinforces confidence that GadgetShare can handle the unpredictable ebb and flow of peer-to-peer rentals without skipping a beat.

HEART Framework and Success Metrics

HEART Framework Metrics

To translate vision into measurable outcomes, the GadgetShare's team aligned each HEART dimension with specific, quantifiable KPIs:

Dimension	KPI	Definition
Happiness	Net Promoter Score (NPS)	Owners' likelihood to recommend GadgetShare, measured on a 0–10 scale.
	Average Rental Rating	Aggregate renter satisfaction based on device condition and handoff ease.
Engagement	Monthly Active Renters	Count of unique users completing at least one rental per month.
	Session Frequency	Average number of app sessions per user each week.
Adoption	Weekly New Renters	Number of first-time renters onboarded each week.
	Owner Onboarding Rate	Percentage of owners who complete profile creation and listing setup.
Retention	30-Day Repeat Rate	Percentage of renters returning to rent again within 30 days.
	Owner Churn Rate	Percentage of owners inactive for over 60 days.

Task Success	Booking Completion Rate	Ratio of successful bookings to initiated rental requests.
	Average Confirmation Time	Average time elapsed from renter request to owner approval.

In the above chart,

- The **Happiness** metric captures qualitative sentiment; GadgetShare surveys every user post-rental and tracks changes over time.
- **Engagement** and **Adoption** measure the scale of the people that are actively using the service and how quickly new hosts/renters come aboard.
- **Retention** ensures that once people try the platform, they keep coming back.
- **Task Success** focuses on the critical user journey, booking to return, measuring both completion rates and flow efficiency.

This HEART-aligned dashboard gives GadgetShare a balanced view of user experience, platform growth, and operational quality, all in a single glance.

Operational and Financial Indicators

An effective connection between product initiatives and business outcomes depends on choosing metrics that translate team efforts into real-world impact. A focus on operational and financial indicators ensures that every experiment, feature rollout, or UX tweak can be tied back to tangible performance shifts. The clarity on KPIs, how it's calculated, what insight it delivers, and which teams own it, provides a shared language for prioritization and alignment. Below, a layout breaks down five key measures that illustrate how tracking these numbers drove targeted actions and lifted results.

Indicator	Calculation	What It Reveals
Gadget Utilization Rate	Days rented ÷ days listed per device	Identification of high-demand vs. idle inventory, guiding stocking choices

Revenue per User (RPU)	Monthly rental income ÷ active users	Individual customer value, informing loyalty offers and marketing spend
Average Order Value (AOV)	Total revenue ÷ number of bookings	Effectiveness of pricing, upsell and bundling strategies
Marketplace Liquidity	Pending rental requests ÷ available devices per region	Supply-demand balance signals, prompting targeted supply boosts or promos
Operational Throughput	Completed rentals per hour	Backend efficiency gauge, helping teams optimize workflows and capacity

Tying features and experiments directly to these metrics ensured cross-functional alignment. For example, a drop in Marketplace Liquidity across rural zones triggered a series of localized demo events run by partnerships with community centers. That effort expanded device availability by 30 percent, restoring balance between requests and listings and reducing wait times.

Similarly, when AOV edged downward, UX designers refocused checkout flows to streamline add-on selection and clarify bundle pricing. The resulting changes elevated average spend per booking, validating the use of targeted design sprints tied to specific KPI movements.

Sample OKRs and Reviews

The above so far planned roadmap linked quarterly objectives to KPI targets. A Q1 example is as below:

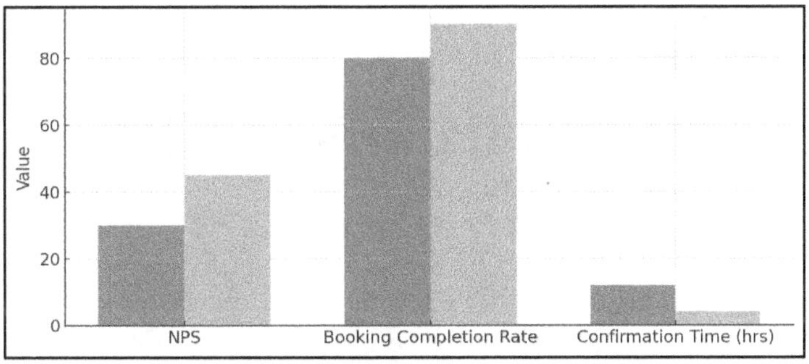

Fig 1.2 Q1 Baseline vs. Target

The bar chart above plots each metric's starting point against its Q1 goal, making it easy to see where the biggest leaps are expected and helping the team track progress at a glance.

Below is a concise view of the Q1 objectives and targets, alongside a quick-reference chart of baseline vs target values:

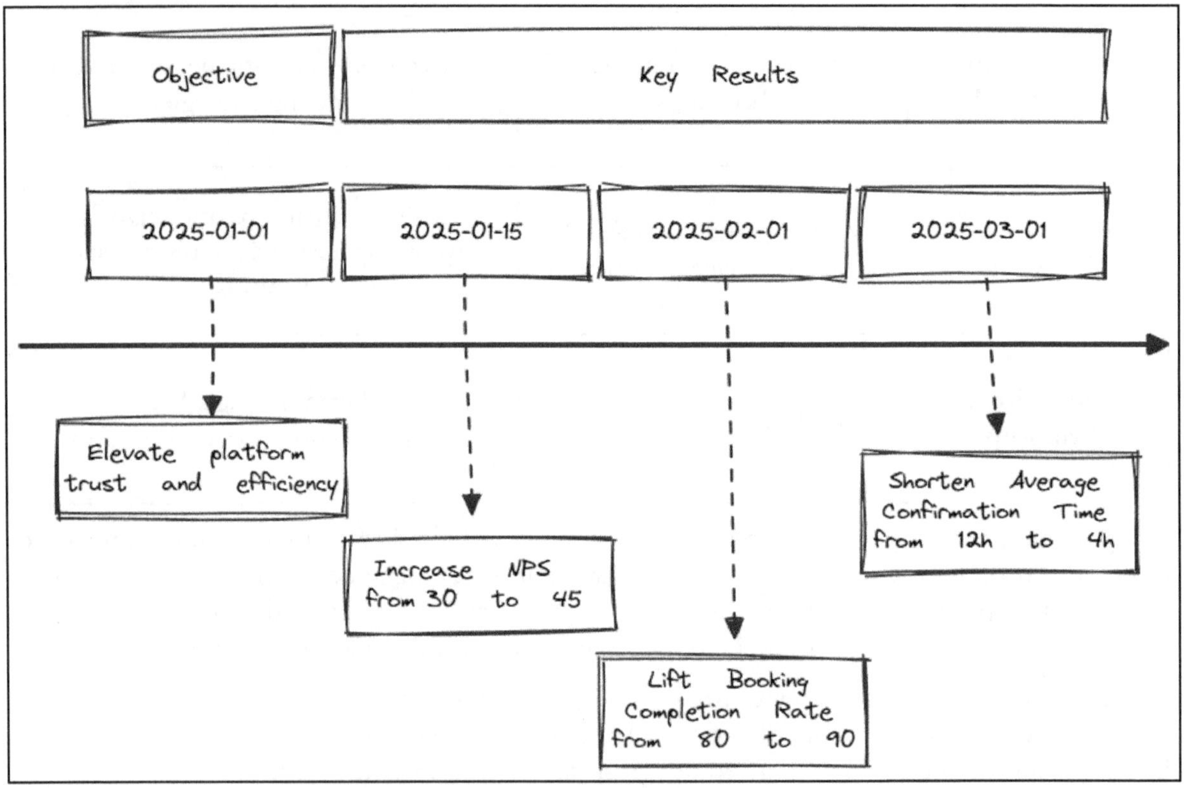

Fig 1.3 Q1 OKRs – Platform Trust & Efficiency

In their daily stand-up meetings, the team checked dashboards that combined HEART and financial metrics to quickly test assumptions and refine priorities. And in weekly leadership reviews, these insights guided tactical adjustments, making sure each sprint brought steady progress toward GadgetShare's vision.

Cross-Functional Collaboration Rituals

From early pilot launches through full-scale rollout, the GadgetShare's success hinged on tight coordination between engineering, design, operations and customer support. To foster this collaboration, the founding team introduced a mix of recurring standups, ad-hoc backlog workshops and active sync sessions, each purpose-built to surface dependencies, resolve blockers and reinforce shared ownership.

Daily Cross-Team Standups

Now here, rather than siloed team huddles, the GadgetShare adopted a single, short daily standup with representation from every function: one engineer, one designer, one operations lead and one support representative. Each attendee shared three quick points, progress since yesterday, planned work today and any emerging issues. By hearing each other's updates side by side, teams gained immediate visibility into interlocking tasks, from new UI components waiting on API changes to support tickets highlighting usability gaps. A strict five-minute timer kept discussions focused, and a shared digital board captured action items in real time.

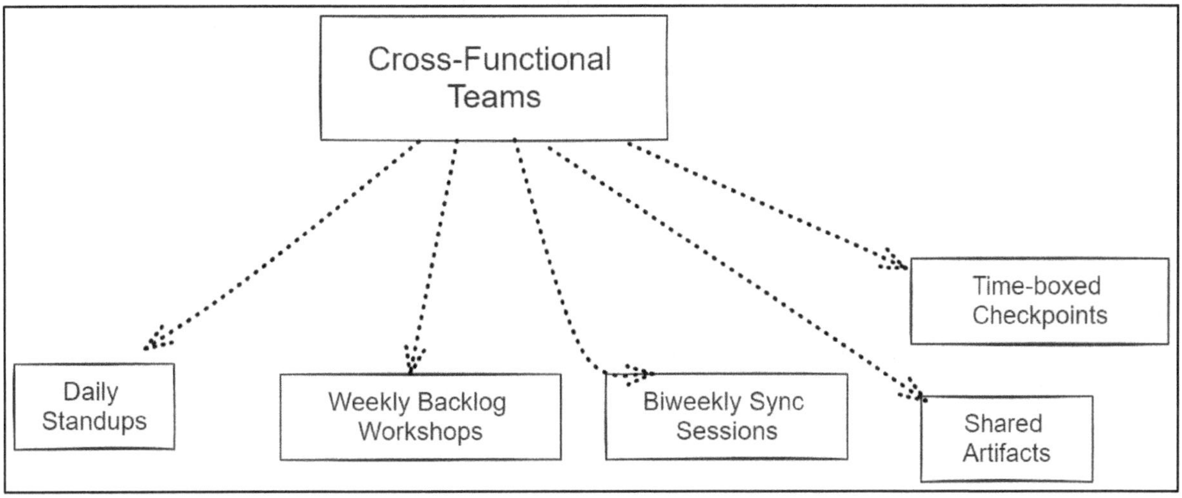

Fig 1.4 Cross-Functional Collaboration Rituals

Weekly Backlog Workshops

Once a week, product managers convened an ad-hoc backlog workshop to refine and prioritize upcoming features. These two-hour sessions began with a quick review of key metrics, such as booking completion rate and session frequency, to ground decisions in data. Next, cross-functional stakeholders collaboratively evaluated new requests or bug reports, assigning RICE scores and clarifying acceptance criteria. Designers sketched flows on virtual whiteboards, engineers estimated technical effort and operations flagged potential logistic impacts. The time-boxing of each backlog item discussion to ten minutes helped the team with balanced thoroughness with efficiency, ensuring the backlog remained both relevant and actionable.

Biweekly Sync Sessions

To align on longer-term initiative progress, the GadgetShare held biweekly sync sessions that alternated focus between feature roadmaps and infrastructure improvements. During feature syncs, engineering demos brought UX prototypes to life, inviting rapid feedback from support and operations on edge cases or process constraints. Infrastructure syncs spotlighted upcoming deployments, such as database replicas or new container clusters, allowing design and support teams to prepare updated documentation and customer-facing guides. These sessions deepened mutual understanding of technical trade-offs and ensured every function stayed ahead of planned changes.

Shared Artifacts and Collaboration Tools

Central to these rituals was a living set of shared artifacts: a unified product roadmap, a collaborative design library, a prioritized backlog board and a deployment calendar. Hosted in a cloud workspace, these artifacts served as single sources of truth. Change notifications, triggered by issue tracker updates or code merges, alerted relevant stakeholders, reducing email noise and preventing miscommunication. Additionally, a dedicated #collaboration Slack channel captured quick Q&A threads and linked to updated documents, preserving context for asynchronous team members.

Time-Boxed Checkpoints and Continuous Feedback

Recognizing that open-ended meetings erode momentum, all ceremonies began and ended on schedule. Pre-meeting agendas circulated 24 hours in advance, with clear goals and required pre-reads. At the close of each ritual, a two-minute retrospective solicited one "start" and one "stop" suggestion, ensuring every session evolved to better serve the team. These checkpoints reinforced a culture of continuous improvement, where collaboration itself became a dynamic, fine-tuned process.

All these activities or the rituals really boosted the cross-team coordination and helped the GadgetShare team meet deadlines consistently, keeping everyone focused on delivering value without unnecessary delays.

Iteration Workflow and Release Planning

Drawing on proven iteration workflows, the GadgetShare adopted a two-week sprint cycle to balance steady progress with responsiveness. This cadence created predictable delivery rhythms, enabling the team to commit to clear goals while remaining flexible to change.

Predictable Sprint Cadence

Each sprint began with a concise planning session. On Monday mornings, the product manager reviewed the highest-priority backlog items, tied to current KPIs, with engineers, designers and support staff. Together, they assessed capacity and complexity, locking the sprint's scope and deferring unplanned work to a dedicated buffer queue. This approach focused the team on sprint goals while preserving agility for urgent issues.

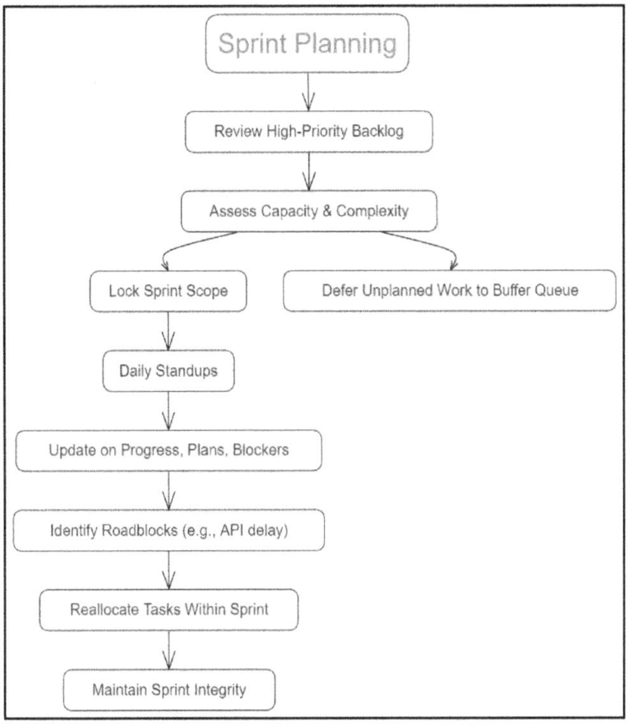

Fig 1.5 Sprint Cadence

Daily standups provided a brief forum for updates on completed tasks, planned work and emerging blockers. When an unexpected roadblock, such as a delayed API change, arose, team members reallocated tasks within the sprint, swapping lower-priority stories for unblocked work. This real-time rebalancing kept progress on track without compromising the sprint's integrity.

Rigorous Backlog Refinement

The team had a one-hour backlog refinement workshop every Thursday afternoon. Folks from different teams looked at the top ten backlog stories, using recent metric trends to guide the discussions. There were engineers who gave some rough estimates of the effort, designers who presented wireframes or mockups, and operations who talked about potential infrastructure or logistics concerns.

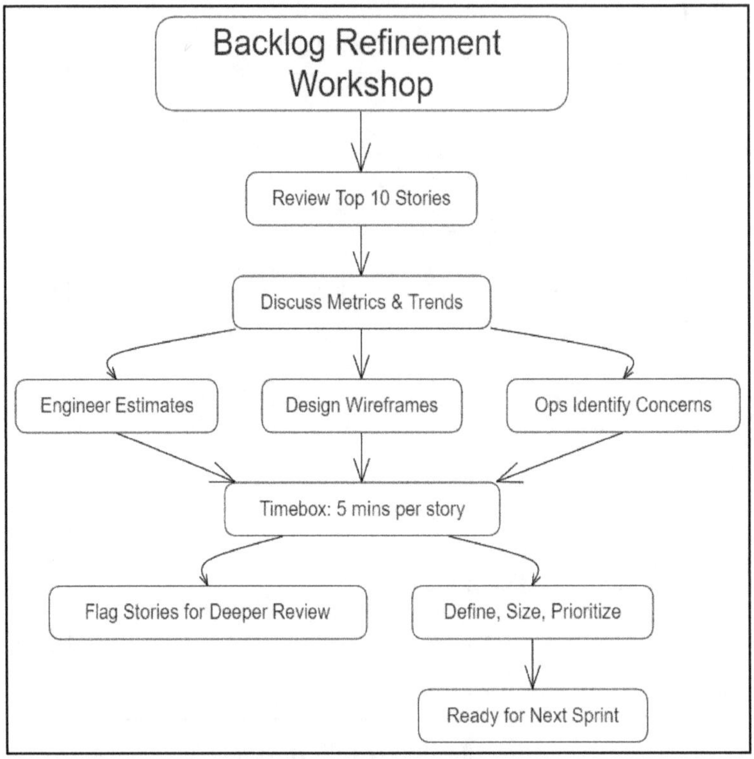

Fig 1.6 Backlog Refining

We timeboxed each story discussion to five minutes, and it went really well. Stories that needed more technical analysis were scheduled for follow-up architectural reviews. By the time the workshop ended, we had clearly defined, sized, and ordered our stories by priority, so they were all set for selection in the next sprint.

Release Candidate Criteria

To maintain quality, every feature branch underwent automated unit and integration tests before merging. Passing builds deployed automatically to a staging environment for end-to-end smoke tests covering critical flows: account creation, device search, booking and payment.

Release candidates met three core criteria:

1. New code modules achieved a minimum of 80% coverage.
2. No high-severity bugs remained open for affected functionality.
3. Key endpoints responded in under 200ms under standard load.

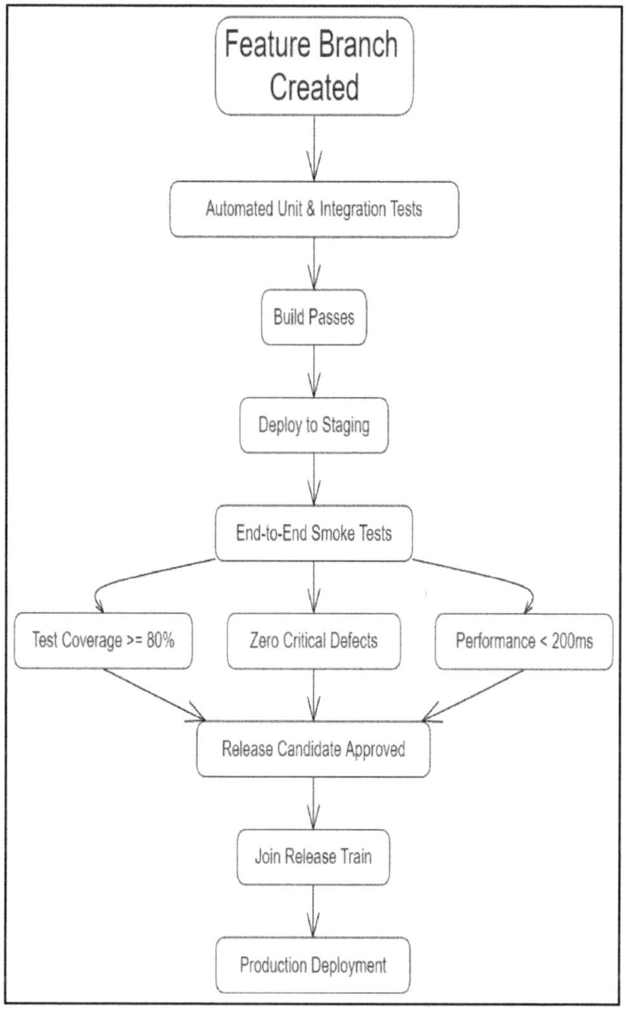

Fig 1.7 Candidate Release Process

The qualified candidates then joined the staging "release train," grouping multiple features for the next production deployment.

Regression-Test Checkpoints

We run a regression suite every night against the staging release train to validate core user scenarios. If there was a failure, it would trigger an alert and rollback, which let us resolve the issue quickly before the next business day.

We did smoke tests on our production environments after each deployment, and we monitored error rates and response times. The alerts flowed into the operations dashboard, providing round-the-clock visibility and reducing time-to-detect regressions.

Rollback Plans and Emergency Fixes

For every production release, a rollback playbook specified the exact Git commit to revert, database rollback commands and communication steps for support and operations. In critical incidents, such as a payment gateway outage, the team executed a fast-track hotfix process, merging minimal patches through accelerated CI checks and smoke tests. Post-mortems documented root causes and updated sprint plans to prevent recurrence.

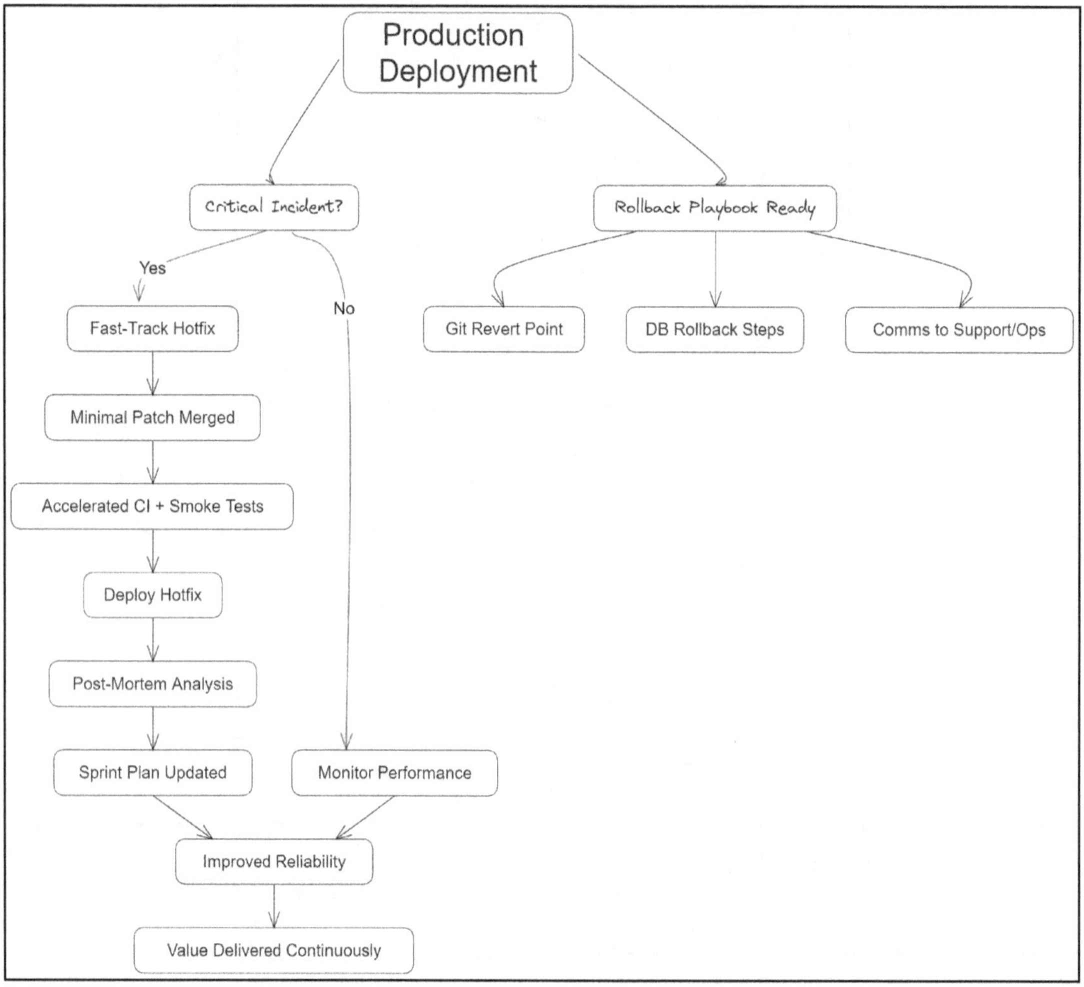

Fig 1.8 Emergency and Rollback Plans

They've got a pretty solid system going on, with a steady sprint rhythm, keeping their backlog in check, strict release gates, automated regression testing, and clear rollback protocols. It's a good mix of keeping things moving and making sure everything's solid. The teams delivered incremental value each sprint with confidence, ensuring robust performance and supporting the platform's promise of seamless, trustworthy gadget sharing.

Adapting to Infrastructure Limits

Following several release cycles, the GadgetShare founders recalled a case study from a growing startup they admired, where teams gathered informally around whiteboards to share real-time insights. Inspired by that example, later recognized as part of the Crystal Agile approach, they designed this strategy session around lightweight collaboration, frequent communication, reflective learning and adaptive planning.

Constraint Decision Audit

The facilitators led the group through a walk-through of past sprints, highlighting where infrastructure limitations, such as API latency and database contention, forced scope reductions or altered feature designs. Visual timelines and incident dashboards provided concrete examples of where delivery speed had been prioritized over completeness or where stability had prevailed at the cost of new enhancements.

In pairs, the product managers and engineers discussed specific decision points. One pair examined the choice to defer automated index tuning for a faster release, while another evaluated the impact of merging multiple features into a single sprint to minimize integration overhead. Each pair documented lessons learned and potential mitigation strategies.

Learnings Documentation

Using an online Kanban board, participants categorized insights under three headings: "Scope Adjustments," "Quality Trade-Offs" and "Velocity Constraints." Each card captured a description of the decision, its outcome metrics (e.g., increased performance issues or reduced deployment time) and recommended actions for future sprints.

Inspired by Crystal's focus on osmotic communication and frequent delivery, the team noted that closer seating, or virtual open channels, could have surfaced performance warnings earlier. They also realized that embedding a lightweight "pre-merge smoke test" step might have avoided a major rollback incident.

Incremental Upgrades

From the learning board, product managers extracted upgrade proposals, such as introducing an API gateway cache layer, automating index rebuilds and integrating a canary-release strategy. Each proposal included a rough effort estimate and an expected impact on KPIs like booking completion and API response times.

Applying Crystal's emphasis on human power and reflective improvement, the group voted on the top three upgrades for the next release cycle. These items entered a dedicated "Infrastructure Sprint" in the backlog, ensuring focused attention alongside feature work.

Mapping Trade-Offs

The facilitators introduced a simple 2×2 matrix mapping scope (feature completeness) against quality (system stability), with delivery speed as a sliding scale. For each proposed upgrade, attendees plotted its likely position in the matrix, discussed acceptable compromise zones and annotated scenarios where pushing speed might yield more strategic value.

Emphasizing Crystal's principle of frequent reflection, the team agreed to embed biweekly mini-retrospects on infrastructure work, ensuring ongoing calibration of trade-off decisions rather than leaving them solely to quarter-end reviews.

This whole case study illustrates how a user-centric, data-informed strategy can guide a concept from spark to scale. By listening to community conversations in social media, validating through structured surveys and mapping usage patterns with heat maps, the GadgetShare built a product founded on real needs. A phased technical roadmap, strengthening core infrastructure, scaling with containers and preparing for serverless growth, showed how to balance speed with stability. The success metrics through the HEART framework aligned the team around key outcomes. The complementary financial and operational metrics, such as gadget utilization rate and marketplace liquidity ensured every decision drove business value. And, the cross-functional rituals and disciplined sprint workflows forged transparent communication, while lightweight Agile reflections inspired by Crystal reinforced continuous adaptation.

Case-Study Freebies

To accelerate your GadgetShare journey, we're offering a set of ready-to-use assets that blend strategic planning with hands-on execution. These templates and frameworks can be imported into Miro, Notion, Excel or your favorite PM tool, then tailored to your team's specific workflows.

Interactive Roadmap Canvas

An interactive roadmap canvas is a visual planner that lets you drag and drop feature buckets, timeboxes and milestones onto a shared board. You can click into any item to update status, add notes or adjust priorities, then see how changes ripple across quarters and sprints. It turns static plans into a living schedule where your whole team can stay in sync and make real-time decisions.

Feature Bucket	Q1 Timebox	Q2 Timebox	Q3 Timebox	Milestone Flag
Core Sharing Flow	Jan–Mar: MVP Launch	Apr–Jun: Scale Tests	Jul–Sep: Feature Harden	v1 Launch (Mar 31)

Reputation Engine	Jan–Mar: Design Sprint	Apr–Jun: Development	Jul–Sep: Public Beta	Beta Release (Jun 30)
Delivery Options	Jan–Mar: Pilot Routes	Apr–Jun: Expand Zones	Jul–Sep: Automate Ops	Courier Integration (Jul 15)
Analytics Dashboard	Jan–Mar: Scoping & UX	Apr–Jun: Prototype	Jul–Sep: Rollout	Dashboard v1 (Sep 30)

You can rename buckets to match your pillars, click a header and swap in something like "Onboarding Magic" or "Revenue Boosters," so every feature lands in the right place. **You can tweak timeboxes** to mirror your calendar, shift Q1 to July–September, stretch sprints to three weeks or shrink them to one. When columns line up with real dates, planning feels less theoretical and more like tomorrow's to-do list. **You can flag milestones** with bold text, colored dots or even an emoji (🚀 for launch!). A quick glance shows everyone where beta builds, public rollouts or big integrations sit on the timeline.

You can score priorities by adding a "RICE" column. Plug in Reach, Impact, Confidence and Effort values, then sort so the highest-value work bubbles up. **You can highlight risks** with a Red/Amber/Green tag next to each feature. High-uncertainty items jump off the page, reminding you to carve out buffer time or plan fallbacks. **You can bake in check-ins** by inserting rows for sprint reviews or quarterly huddles. List who's attending and what you'll demo, so feedback loops stay tight and nobody's left guessing.

Priority & Risk Tracker

It's a dynamic table where you list each feature alongside its RICE score (Reach, Impact, Confidence, Effort) and a Red/Amber/Green risk flag. Clicking any row lets you tweak scores, jot down blockers or dependencies, and instantly sort by top impact or highest risk, so nothing sneaks up on your next sprint.

Initiative	RICE Score	Risk Level	Mitigation Tactics	Owner	Status

Expand Courier Delivery	90	Medium	Secure 3 vendor contracts; test 2 regions	Operations Lead	In Progress
Automate DB Indexing	75	High	Schedule off-peak updates; add alerts	DevOps Lead	Planned
Launch Loyalty Program	60	Low	A/B test rewards; gather early feedback	Product Manager	Not Started
Introduce Review Badges	55	Low	Validate badges UX; phase rollout	UX Designer	Completed

When you sort the table by RICE Score, your highest-value ideas float to the top. That way, you and the team instantly see which experiments or features promise the biggest payoff. As soon as a new item lands in the backlog, just click the "RICE" header and watch the list reorder, no more hunting through dozens of rows for your next big win. In your weekly standup, glance at the Risk column and call out any Reds or Ambers. If something moved from Green to Amber, note what's changed and assign a quick mitigation task on the spot.

Next, then pick someone to shepherd each initiative from idea through launch. Populate an "Owner" field so there's zero confusion about who's responsible for gathering feedback, unblocking dependencies or raising flags. When accountability lives in the same row as your feature details, every request and update has a clear point of contact. And finally, add a "Status" column with flavors like Not Started, In Progress and Completed. Color-code those labels or use simple icons so anyone scanning the canvas knows exactly where you stand. You'll spot stalled work at a glance, and it's easy to share progress snapshots with stakeholders without exporting to another tool.

External Template Resources

For a wider range of ready-to-use assets, roadmap canvases, risk registers, prioritization spreadsheets and collaboration boards, explore these reputable sources:

- **Miro Template Gallery** https://miro.com/templates/
- **Lucidchart Templates** https://www.lucidchart.com/pages/templates

- **Notion Template Gallery** https://www.notion.so/templates
- **Smartsheet Template Center** https://www.smartsheet.com/templates
- **Airtable Universe** https://www.airtable.com/universe/latest

All these platforms provide robust, professionally designed templates that you can import and tailor to your GadgetShare workflow, saving setup time and ensuring best practices.

EMPOWERING WOMEN VIA MOBILE EXPERIENCE

One evening, the Sakhi's founder, Priya Sharma, paused during a carpool chat to think about her own challenges. She was juggling video conferences, coordinating childcare, and looking for good mentors, all on the same device. The existing platforms felt impersonal and didn't take into account the cultural nuances and privacy considerations that were important to her community. That's when Sakhi got the idea to create a mobile experience focused on women, where they could connect, learn, and grow in safe, supportive spaces.

The market data backed up Priya's gut feeling. Surveys showed that more than 85% of urban women aged 22 to 35 in major cities have smartphones, but few apps meet their professional and cultural needs. Rural homemakers and students faced some barriers too, but the team decided to focus first on Young Urban Professionals. These are digitally literate women with stable incomes, active social networks, and a strong desire to develop their careers. Field visits to startup hubs, interviews at incubators, and analysis of app usage trends helped inform this decision, revealing critical factors like preferred device budgets, language preferences, and social norms that would shape Sakhi's persona framework with precision.

Persona Mapping and Cultural Requirements

Selecting Target Persona

After evaluating multiple segments, rural homemakers, engineering students and urban entrepreneurs, the team zeroed in on the Young Urban Professional (YUP) persona. YUPs, typically women in their late twenties working full-time in corporate or startup environments, showed strong digital literacy and an appetite for professional growth. In discussions at mentoring meetups, these women expressed frustration with generic networking platforms that failed to account for privacy concerns and cultural etiquette. They desired mentorship opportunities tailored to female voices, localized event recommendations and resources framed in both English and regional languages. By focusing on this segment, the Sakhi could deliver immediate value, refining features such as one-click event RSVPs, in-app messaging with verified mentors and content filters aligned with professional interests.

Assessing Cultural Sensitivities

The interviews showed that there were some complex cultural requirements. For example, in Delhi and Mumbai, English was the main language people used, but users also liked key terms in Hindi or Marathi, especially for event titles and mentor bios. In cities like Bengaluru and Chennai, people were using code-switching, that is, switching between English and local languages like Kannada or Tamil, a lot in their social media groups. This shows that there's a demand for push notifications that are available in more than one language. Privacy was a top priority, and several YUPs asked for anonymous posting options in discussion forums to avoid workplace gossip. The decision to implement granular privacy controls, like pseudonymous profiles and opt-in location sharing for in-person meetups, was driven by these insights.

Device Budget and Connectivity Patterns

The analysis of market data showed that most YUPs owned mid-range Android devices with 3–4 GB of RAM, prioritizing battery life and 4G connectivity. Wi-Fi access clustered in office campuses and cafés, whereas home networks varied in reliability. To accommodate intermittent connectivity, the Sakhi's design team incorporated offline caching for event listings and mentorship content. Media assets, like short video tutorials, auto-compressed to reduce data usage. App performance benchmarks ensured launch times under two seconds on 4G connections and graceful degradation on 3G networks, preserving the user experience across fluctuating bandwidth conditions.

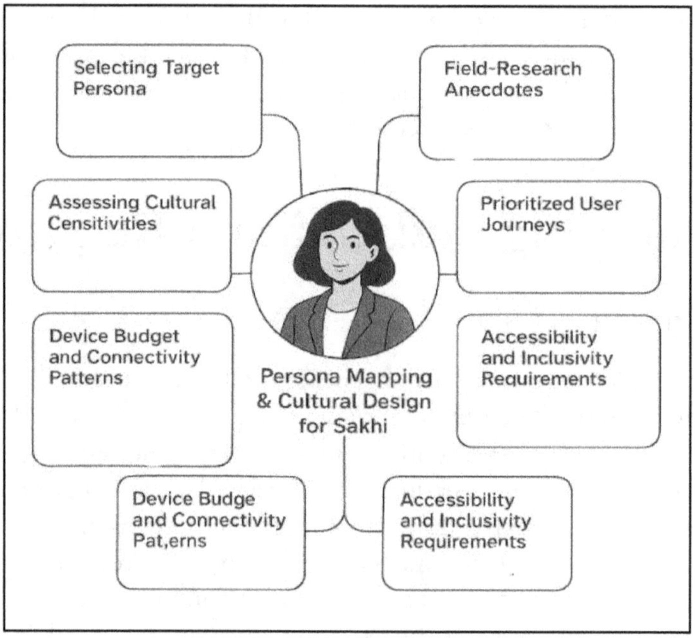

Fig 2.1 Persona Mapping

Field-Research Anecdotes

While they were doing fieldwork at a women's entrepreneurship summit, they saw that a lot of people were crowding around a single booth to register, which led to long lines and a lot of frustration. On the other hand, using an app for digital RSVPs cut down on wait times and let organizers send out timely reminders. In a different focus group, people really liked the idea of a mentorship directory, but they said it was important to have profiles that had been checked by someone to keep people trusting the directory. These stories highlighted the need for smooth event planning and reliable trust tools, which led to the creation of a mentor verification badge and an instant calendar sync.

Prioritized User Journeys

The team put all these insights together to create a map of the top user journeys for Sakhi's MVP: finding nearby workshops, sending mentor chat requests, saving relevant resources, and joining discussion circles based on shared interests. Each journey had micro-interactions like one-tap language toggles and contextual tooltips explaining privacy settings. Wireframes showed these flows, with placeholders for regional language versions and accessibility checks for font size and contrast ratios, making sure it was easy for users to read.

Accessibility and Inclusivity Requirements

It's all about meeting accessibility standards, so Sakhi added screen-reader labels, high-contrast themes, and you can adjust the text size. We know that some YUPs might need to use voice inputs on the go, so we made it so you can post and search hands-free with voice-to-text. They made sure to include different cultures in terms of color schemes and iconography. They had local illustrations for events like Diwali, Navratri, and Christmas, which helped bring people together in India's cities.

The focus on the Young Urban Professional segment, which was based on quantitative device data, field anecdotes, and detailed journey mapping, let Sakhi develop features that really resonated with its initial users. The rest of the chapters build on that, talking about technical architecture, success metrics, and collaborative processes designed around Sakhi's mission.

Platform and Security Architecture

Modular Service Design

With all the info about the users and their culture, Priya Sharma and her engineering co-founders came up with a solid architecture based on what the users needed. They sketched Sakhi's infrastructure on a whiteboard, dividing the application into four modular microservices, Authentication, Event Management, Messaging and Content Delivery, each encapsulated in its own container to allow independent updates and minimize disruption.

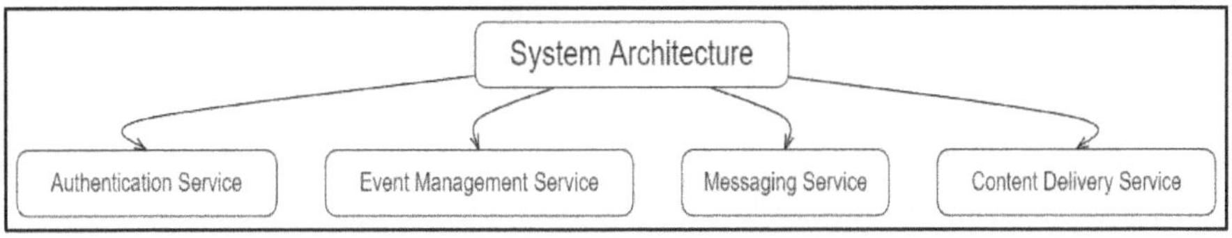

Fig 2.2 Simple Architecture

Authentication Service

The team built a dedicated microservice responsible for one-time-password (OTP) login flows and session management. To accommodate sudden spikes, such as mass event registrations, they designed the service to be stateless, relying on a distributed in-memory store for temporary session data. Horizontal scaling across Kubernetes pods ensured that SMS gateway integrations remained reliable, even under high traffic. Feature flags enabled controlled rollout of advanced security options, such as biometric fallback, without redeploying the entire service.

Event Management Service

A separate microservice stored details for workshops, panel discussions and mentorship meetups. Recognizing that many YUP users faced flaky home connections, engineers introduced offline caching: the service generated signed, encrypted snapshots of nearby events, which mobile clients stored locally. When connectivity resumed, the service reconciled the cached data with updates from the server. This design improved discovery reliability, while background sync jobs performed delta updates to limit data transfer and preserve battery life.

Messaging Service

Mentor-mentee conversations required both security and efficiency. The team implemented end-to-end encryption using a double-ratchet protocol, with ephemeral message queues to reduce on-device retention. Deleted messages were scrubbed from both client and server logs after expiration, aligning with privacy preferences expressed during persona interviews. The service auto-scaled based on queue depth metrics, ensuring low latency even during peak mentoring hours.

Content Delivery Service

Articles, video tutorials and push notifications streamed through a CDN-backed microservice. Engineers configured regional edge caches to serve major metros, while fallback logic rerouted requests through central nodes in less connected regions. Adaptive bitrate streaming for videos balanced quality with network constraints. A/B experiments on content load strategies, such as prefetching versus on-demand, ran in parallel, guiding iterative performance tuning based on real user metrics.

Security Foundations and OWASP Practices

One of Sakhi's main focuses was security, and they used the OWASP Mobile Security Project to set a solid, industry-standard baseline. The team started by creating a detailed threat model, mapping out potential vulnerabilities across data-at-rest, data-in-transit, and client-server interactions. They put risks into categories like insecure local storage, weak session controls, and injection attacks, and gave each one a level of severity, making sure they focused on the most critical threats.

From that groundwork, several key controls emerged. A few standout security measures took shape:

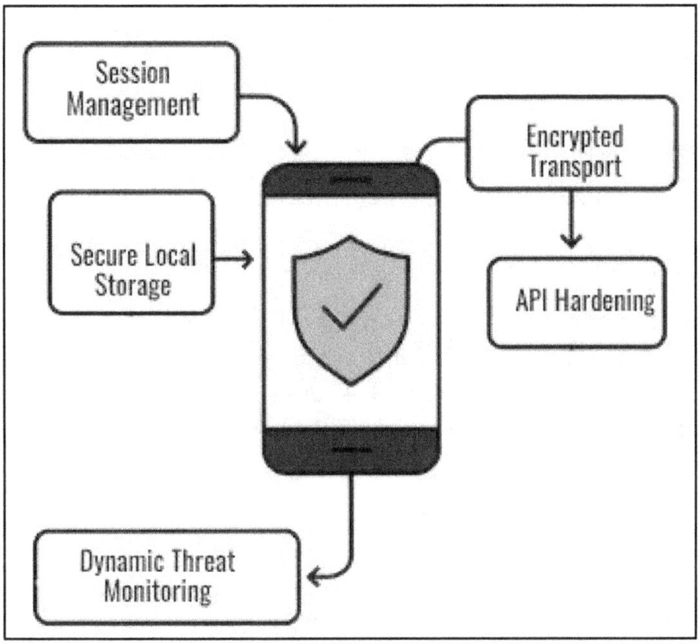

Fig 2.3 OWASP Security Controls

Encrypted Transport

All traffic runs over TLS 1.3 with top-tier ciphers. The mobile app pins its certificate, so any server that doesn't match the known public key gets blocked immediately.

API Hardening

An OWASP-approved validation library lives at the gateway, scrubbing every incoming field to stop injection attacks. Rate limits and IP throttles guard against brute-force and DDoS attempts.

Secure Local Storage

Keys stay locked in Android Keystore or iOS Keychain. User data in SQLite is encrypted with per-session keys generated during the OTP handshake, so nothing can be read outside an authenticated session.

Session Management

Short-lived JWTs handle auth, with rotating refresh tokens for seamless yet safe re-entry. Sensitive user details never travel in the token, those stay on the server.

Dynamic Threat Monitoring

A lightweight RASP agent watches for odd API calls or file-tampering attempts. If it spots anything suspicious, it automatically disables risky features and raises an alert.

By applying OWASP best practices at every layer, network, API, storage and client, the team built a security posture that adapts as new threats emerge.

Navigating Trade-Offs

Each architectural decision balanced competing constraints:

On-Device Storage vs. Responsiveness

Local storage caps hover around 50 MB to prevent the app from ballooning on users' devices. Stale records automatically roll off after a configurable time-to-live, so only the most recent and mission-critical data remains available offline. It keeps initial load times snappy while ensuring users in low-connectivity zones always have exactly what they need at their fingertips.

Network Usage vs. Freshness

Sync schedules adapt in real time to where your users are and how often they interact. In high-traffic regions, background fetches fire every few minutes; in spotty signal areas, those intervals stretch out, conserving bandwidth and battery life. Under the hood, usage patterns feed a predictive model that anticipates when fresh data is truly necessary, so you never overfetch or leave users staring at stale information.

Regulatory Compliance vs. Feature Flexibility

Every new permission comes with a clear opt-in prompt that surfaces exactly what the app will do with the data and why. Behind the scenes, a consent ledger timestamps each user's choices, while an audit trail logs any changes to privacy settings. That way, your onboarding flow stays light and focused, yet you retain a bulletproof record that satisfies India's IT Rules 2021 without creating consent fatigue.

With the core architecture in place, the founders planned further enhancements, like introducing Istio for dynamic routing and granular telemetry, enabling real-time insights into inter-service communications. Then, embedding static analysis and dependency audits into CI/CD pipelines using tools like OWASP Dependency-Check to catch vulnerabilities before deployment. And, also to run chaos experiments, such as pod terminations and latency injections, to validate fallback behaviors and ensure uninterrupted user experiences. All these comprehensive architectural and security considerations transformed Sakhi from a concept into a trustworthy, scalable platform. Rooted in persona-driven insights, the design priorities secured both technical robustness and user-centric accessibility, setting the stage for rapid feature evolution and broadening impact.

Feature Prioritization Matrix

After defining core services and securing the platform, Priya Sharma's team turned to prioritizing features under tight resource constraints. They adopted the RICE framework, scoring features by

Reach, Impact, Confidence and Effort, to objectively rank potential functionalities. This approach allowed them to balance user value with technical complexity and align roadmap decisions with both persona needs and business goals.

RICE Framework Overview

- **Reach** estimates how many users will engage with the feature within a set time frame (e.g., number of YUPs likely to use SOS alerts in a month).
- **Impact** gauges the magnitude of benefit each interaction delivers (e.g., improved safety vs. improved engagement).
- **Confidence** reflects the team's certainty in their Reach and Impact estimates, often informed by research or prototypes.
- **Effort** measures the total work required across design, development and QA, expressed in person-weeks.

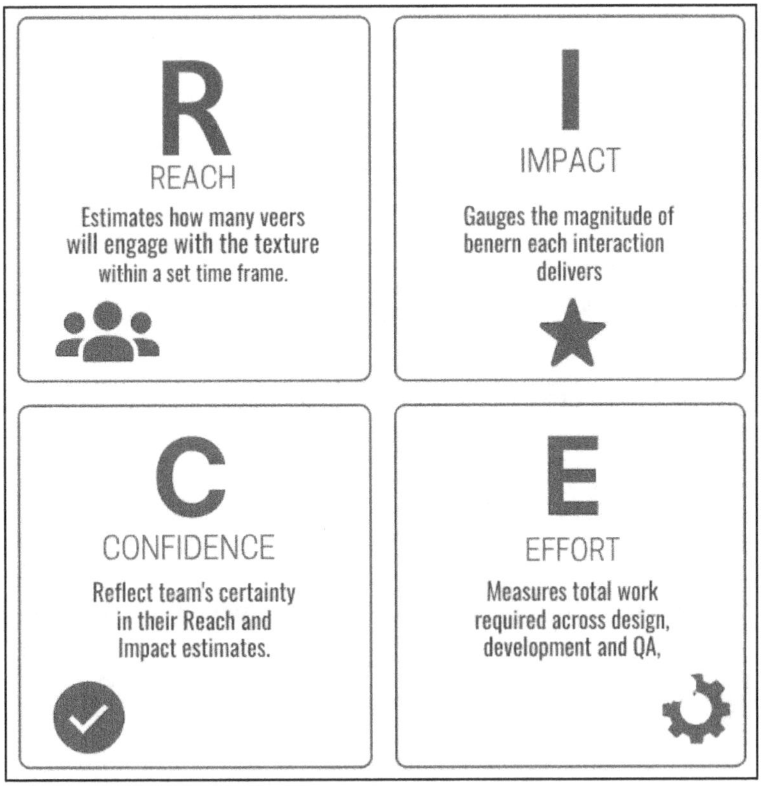

Fig 2.4 RICE Framework

A feature's RICE score equals (Reach × Impact × Confidence) / Effort, yielding a single metric for comparison.

Applying RICE to Sakhi's Feature Set

The team evaluated their initial feature backlog, including SOS alerts, peer-to-peer messaging, location-based meetups and mentor discoverability, through collaborative scoring sessions.

SOS Alerts

- **Reach:** Pilot data suggested 40% of YUPs would use safety alerts at least once per quarter. With an initial user base of 10,000, Reach = 4,000.
- **Impact:** A high-impact feature, rated 3 on a scale of 0.5 (minimal) to 3 (transformative), since it directly enhances personal security.
- **Confidence:** Moderate confidence (60%), based on qualitative interviews highlighting safety concerns but without quantitative usage history.
- **Effort:** Estimated at 8 person-weeks for design, back-end integration with SMS services and front-end testing.

RICE Score: (4,000 × 3 × 0.6) / 8 = 900.

Peer-to-Peer Messaging Encryption

- **Reach:** Messaging anticipated to engage 70% of active users, Reach = 7,000.
- **Impact:** Rated 2, since encrypted chats address privacy but represent an incremental improvement over basic messaging.
- **Confidence:** High (80%), given existing prototypes using open-source encryption libraries.
- **Effort:** 12 person-weeks to integrate double-ratchet protocol, key management and UI flows.

RICE Score: (7,000 × 2 × 0.8) / 12 = 933.

Location-Based Meetups

- **Reach:** 50% of users likely to schedule or attend in-person events monthly, Reach = 5,000.
- **Impact:** Rated 1.5 for increased community engagement but with potential privacy trade-offs.
- **Confidence:** Moderate (50%), research indicated interest but also privacy hesitation.
- **Effort:** 10 person-weeks for map integrations, geofencing and consent flows.

RICE Score: (5,000 × 1.5 × 0.5) / 10 = 375.

Mentor Discoverability Filters

- **Reach:** 80% of users browse mentor listings, Reach = 8,000.
- **Impact:** Rated 2.5, as improved matching significantly enhances user satisfaction.
- **Confidence:** High (85%), based on AB tests of prototype filters.
- **Effort:** 6 person-weeks for UI design, backend filtering logic and recommendation algorithms.

RICE Score: (8,000 × 2.5 × 0.85) / 6 ≈ 2,833.

Prioritization Workshop and Trade-Off Analysis

In a dedicated workshop, cross-functional stakeholders reviewed RICE scores alongside qualitative insights. While Mentor Discoverability topped the list, the team considered strategic trade-offs:

- **Scope vs. Delivery Speed:** SOS Alerts, though lower in RICE than messaging, delivered critical safety value. The team decided to bundle a lightweight SOS prototype in the next sprint, deferring advanced encryption to a later cycle.
- **Quality vs. Effort:** Messaging encryption required extensive QA. To balance velocity, the team split this into a minimum viable variant, secure text only, and a later phase offering media encryption.

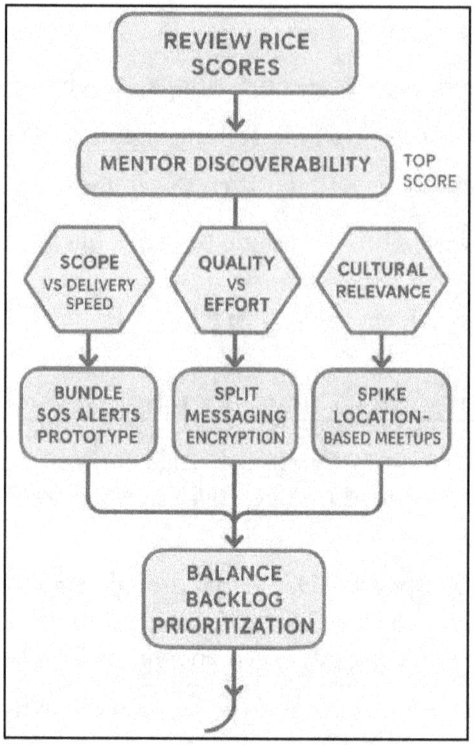

Fig 2.5 RICE-based Prioritization

- **Cultural Relevance:** Location-Based Meetups, despite a lower score, aligned closely with persona cultural needs for safe, in-person community. A side project team began a feasibility spike to ensure compliance with privacy regulations before full implementation.

Roadmap Alignment and Timeboxing

Using the prioritized list, Priya and the PMs placed features into quarterly timeboxes:

Feature	Q1 Timebox	Q2 Timebox	Notes
Mentor Discoverability Filters	Jan–Mar: Build		Highest RICE; drives engagement
Messaging Encryption (MVP)	Jan–Mar: Prototype	Apr–Jun: Harden	MVP for text only; follow-up encryption for media

SOS Alerts (Lightweight)	Jan–Mar: Spike	Apr–Jun: Launch	Basic SMS-based alerts for early feedback
Location-Based Meetups (Spike)	Jan–Mar: Research	Apr–Jun: Pilot	Privacy impact assessment and small-scale user testing

This roadmap balanced high-scoring features with strategic pilots, ensuring the team delivered maximum value while managing risk and complexity.

Iterative Scoring and Continuous Reprioritization

After each release, the team recalculated Reach and Confidence using real usage data. This iterative reprioritization allowed adjustments, features that underperformed in Impact were demoted, while those exceeding expectations gained higher effort allocation.

This whole embedment of the RICE framework into the Sakhi's planning rituals, the team and the Priya very well transformed the subjective debates into transparent, data-driven decisions. It provided them with a clear justification for roadmap choices and aligned every stakeholder on shared priorities. It really helped to accelerate the delivery of impactful features under constrained budgets.

Agile Cadence for Distributed Teams

After solidifying their feature priorities with RICE, Priya Sharma and her distributed team recognized the need for an Agile rhythm tailored to varying connectivity and time zones. They researched remote-first practices employed by successful lean startups and adapted those methods to support team members working from co-working hubs, home offices and mobile hotspots. This new cadence emphasized asynchronous communication, focused feedback loops and lightweight sessions to maintain strong collaboration without overwhelming data costs.

Asynchronous Daily Standups

A rigid 9 AM meeting would exclude engineers in regions with limited bandwidth or high commute times. Instead, the Sakhi adopted asynchronous standups via a lightweight chat channel integrated into their collaboration platform. Each morning, team members posted three bullet-point updates before 11 AM: completed tasks, planned work and blockers. Brief voice notes accompanied complex updates when text felt cumbersome. This thinking ensured that all team members, even those on mobile networks, could participate without the need for continuous high-speed connectivity. Product managers reviewed these updates, flagged critical issues and triaged follow-up actions, preserving clarity while avoiding long video calls.

Lightweight Backlog Refinements

Biweekly backlog refinement sessions occurred over 45 minutes, hosted in a low-bandwidth–optimized video room. To reduce strain on network links, participants in low-connectivity zones dialed in via audio-only, while others shared screens sparingly. Each story's core details, acceptance criteria, dependencies and rough estimates, were documented in a shared, text-based backlog board accessible offline. The facilitator timeboxed discussions to five minutes per item, ensuring rapid consensus. Deeper technical debates were offloaded to asynchronous threads in the issue tracker, where architects and senior engineers exchanged detailed proposals without holding up the refinement meeting.

Biweekly Show-and-Tell Sessions

Every two weeks, the team held a 30-minute show-and-tell to demo completed features to all stakeholders. To minimize video bandwidth, demos relied on pre-recorded walkthroughs uploaded in advance, with live Q&A channels for real-time feedback. Designers narrated interactive prototypes stored in a cloud repository, allowing participants to explore flows independently. Support leads and operations colleagues watched these recordings on demand and contributed comments tagged to specific timestamps. This hybrid model preserved interactive feedback loops without forcing synchronous, high-bandwidth participation.

Collaborative Planning Workshops

Quarterly planning workshops convened the full cross-functional team for three-hour sessions focusing on the upcoming roadmap. Recognizing varying connectivity among participants, the planning document blended text outlines, static wireframes and lightweight polls rather than heavy slide decks. During the workshop, participants voted on feature sequencing through an embedded polling tool optimized for mobile use. Votes triggered real-time visuals, visible even on low-resolution screens. Sprint commitments emerged organically as teams aligned on objectives and capacity, informed by both RICE metrics and recent velocity data.

Rituals for Feedback and Alignment

To sustain momentum between structured ceremonies, the Sakhi implemented several low-overhead sync points:

- A quick, 10-minute audio-only call halfway through each sprint to surface emerging risks and adjust scope as needed.
- A brief channel-based showcase where engineers pinned short videos of new features, prompting asynchronous applause and critique threads.
- Weekly one-question polls capturing team sentiment, connectivity challenges and tooling feedback, allowing managers to spot concerns without lengthy meetings.

Managing Connectivity and Cost Constraints

Acknowledging that many team members used personal data plans, the Sakhi optimized tooling for low-data usage:

- All shared diagrams and prototypes were pre-compressed; images auto-downgraded based on detected bandwidth.
- Detailed design and technical specs favored markdown documents over embedded images, ensuring offline readability and minimal downloads.
- Push alerts for critical updates only, reducing background data consumption and preventing notification fatigue.

By weaving these distributed ceremonies and tools into Sakhi's Agile operations, the team maintained high collaboration and rapid iteration despite bandwidth and geography constraints. Their customized cadence, anchored in asynchronous standups, lightweight refinements and hybrid demos, ensured that every voice was heard, decisions moved forward swiftly and feedback loops remained tight, all while respecting the connectivity limitations of an emerging-market context.

Engagement Metrics Dashboard

After refining agile rituals, Priya Sharma turned her attention to quantifying Sakhi's traction. She convened a dashboard sprint where engineers and analysts collaborated on real-time visualizations to track daily and weekly active users, retention curves and stage-by-stage drop-off rates. These charts would guide feature investments, surface friction points and validate assumptions drawn from persona mapping.

Defining Core Metrics and Data Sources

The team began by cataloging essential engagement indicators aligned to their earlier success metrics. Data sources included:

- **User Events Database** that includes each app interaction, screen views, button taps and form submissions.
- **Authentication Logs** includes recorded OTP requests and successful logins, reflecting access frequency.
- **Survey Module Outputs** includes the captured in-app feedback ratings on a 1–5 scale immediately after feature use.
- And, then the **Backend APIs** that includes the emitted performance and error codes, informing reliability charts.

With these streams flowing into a centralized analytics warehouse (AWS Redshift), the team could construct near real-time views for key audiences: product managers, designers and support leads.

Daily and Weekly Active Users

The first visualization mapped unique user logins over rolling windows:

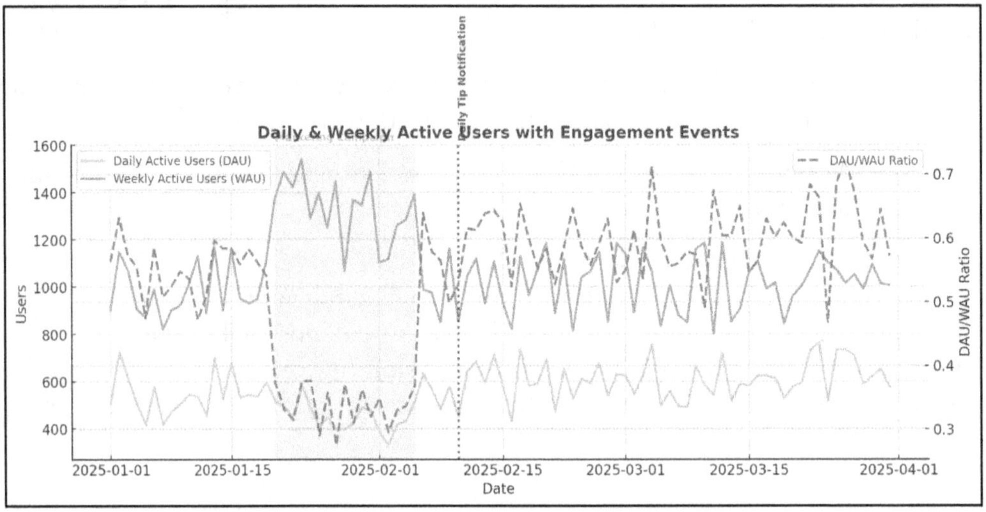

Fig 2.6 DAU/WAU Mapping

In the above chart,

- The Daily Active Users (DAU) is the count of distinct users engaging at least once per day.
- The Weekly Active Users (WAU) is the count over a seven-day sliding window.
- And, the DAU/WAU Ratio is a measure of "stickiness" indicating how often weekly users return daily.

The plotting of DAU and WAU as colored line series on the same time axis revealed engagement trends. Early in Q1, a marketing campaign boosted WAU by 30%, yet DAU/WAU dipped, signaling superficial curiosity rather than habitual use. In response, the PM team introduced a 'daily tip' notification to re-engage users, which uplifted the ratio back to target levels within two weeks.

Retention Curves

To understand cohort behavior, analysts generated retention curves showing the percentage of new users returning on subsequent days and weeks. Each shaded contour represented a signup cohort, with the curve's steepness indicating drop-off velocity.

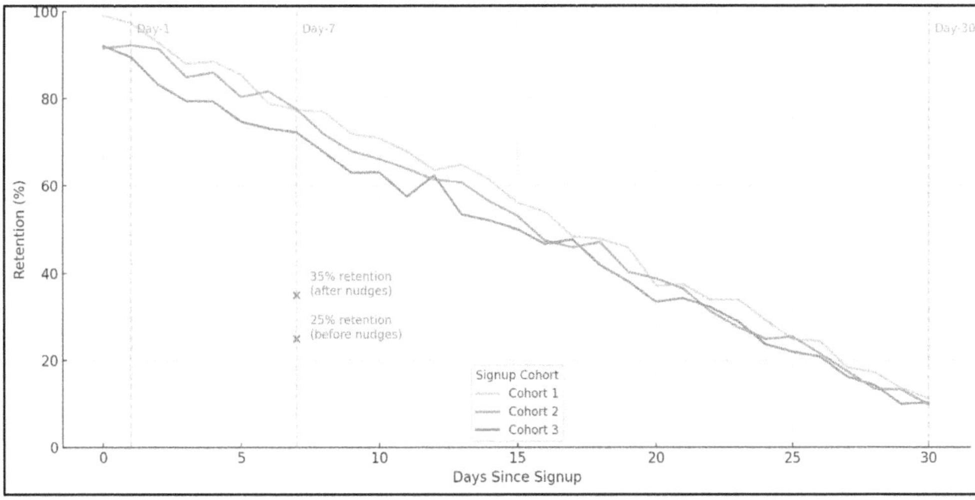

Fig 2.7 Cohort User Retention Curves

In the above chart, you may think of **Day-1 retention** as the first sign that you've made an impression, it's the percentage of people who come back the very next day after signing up. The **Day-7 and Day-30 retention** tell you whether that initial spark turns into a habit, which is crucial for community features like messaging to thrive. When we looked at the data, we noticed something worrying: by Day-7, only about **1 in 4 new users** were still around. That meant people were losing interest before they could really experience the value.

So, we stepped in at just the right moment, **Day-3**, with friendly onboarding tips and mentor suggestions to help users feel connected and find what mattered to them. The result? In A/B tests, Day-7 retention jumped from **25% to 35%**, showing that a well-timed nudge can turn curiosity into commitment.

Funnel Analysis and Drop-Off Rates

Imagine opening the app for the first time and moving step-by-step toward booking a mentor session. The funnel shows how many people make it through each stage:

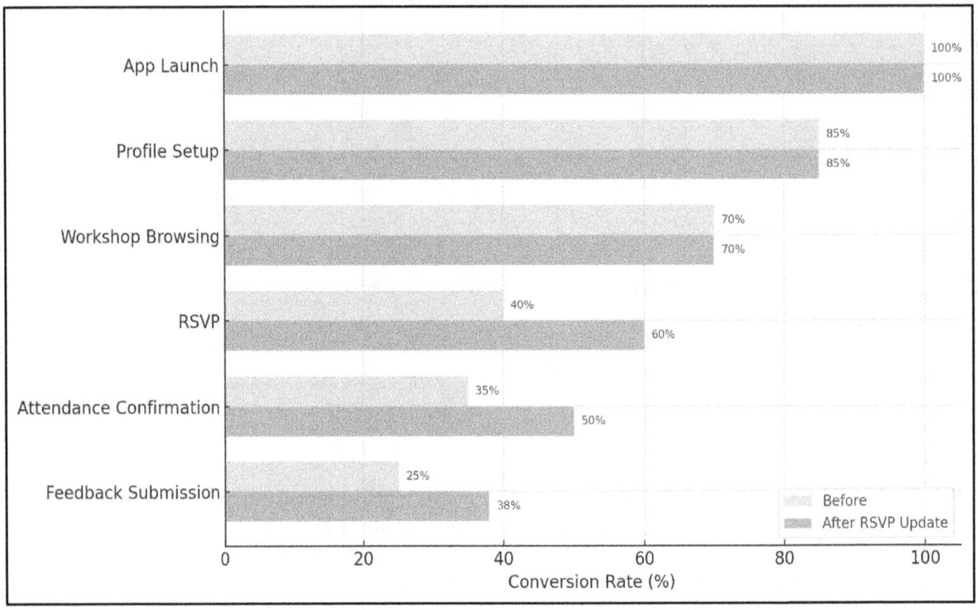

Fig 2.7 User Journey Funnel

In the above funnel,

- From **Launch to Profile Setup** → Most users breeze through, with only a small drop-off.
- From **Setup to Browsing Workshops** → Engagement stays strong, people are curious and start exploring.
- From **Browsing to RSVP** → Here's where the trouble began. Only **4 out of 10** people who looked at an event actually committed to attending. The main culprit? Overloaded event detail pages that slowed people down.
- From **RSVP to Attendance Confirmation** → Fewer still made it to the event, and even fewer left feedback.

To fix the biggest leak, the UX team stripped down the event pages and added a **one-click RSVP button**. The effect was immediate: RSVP conversions jumped from **40% to 60%**, and attendance and feedback rates climbed too. By rethinking just one step, the team turned casual browsers into active participants, making the journey smoother, faster, and more rewarding.

In-App Sentiment Trend

Every week, the Sakhi's team tracked not just how often people used key features, but also how those features made them feel. They plotted **usage volume** and **average sentiment scores** side-by-side for messaging, SOS alerts, and meetups.

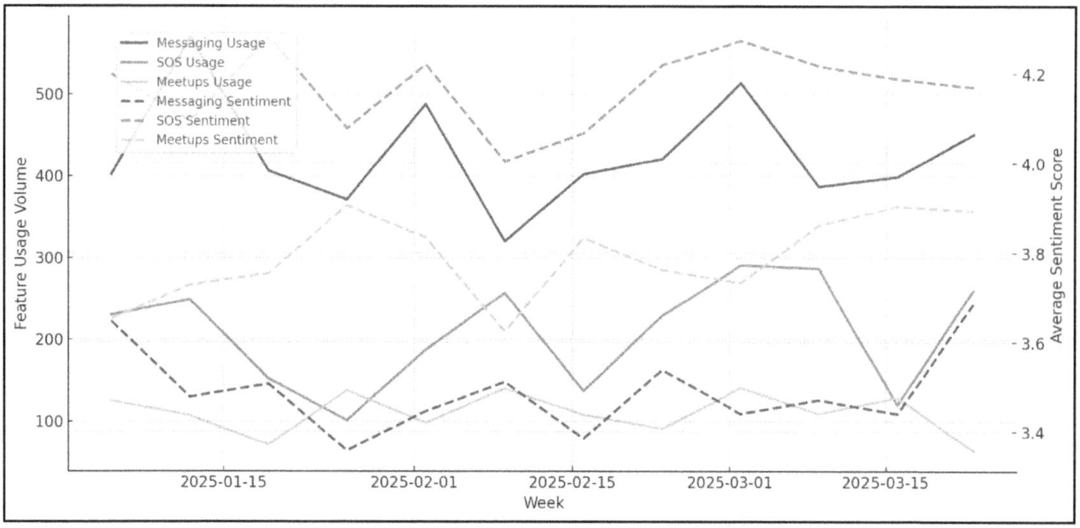

Fig 2.8 In-App Sentiment Trends

A clear pattern emerged: whenever SOS alert usage spiked, so did sentiment, users rated their experience an impressive **4.2 out of 5**. Messaging, while more frequently used, hovered around **3.5**, and meetups sat in the middle at **3.8**.

This was a turning point. Even though SOS alerts scored lower in the RICE prioritization model, the strong emotional value they delivered made them a strategic priority. The team decided to double down on SOS enhancements, knowing it would deepen trust and satisfaction.

All of this lived inside a **Looker dashboard** built for speed and precision:

- **Real-time freshness** → DAU/WAU and funnels updated every 5 minutes, retention curves hourly, sentiment daily.
- **Interactive filters** → Slice data by location, device type, or app version to zero in on specific cohorts, like YUPs in Bengaluru on low-end Android devices.
- **Custom alerts** → Slack pings if DAU dips below 1,000 or Day-1 retention falls under 50%, so the team could respond before issues snowball.

It wasn't just about measuring; it was about turning numbers into stories, and stories into action.

Integrating Feedback Loops

To close the feedback loop between quantitative analytics and qualitative insights, Priya's team embedded in-app micro-surveys at critical funnel exits. Users rating features below 3/5 were prompted to provide open-text feedback. These comments fed into a Tagless AI tool that clustered sentiment themes, "confusing UI," "slow loading," "unclear privacy controls." Analysts surfaced recurring issues in weekly bug-review sessions, directly linking user words to ticket creation.

Researching External Tools

Seeking to streamline analytics, the team evaluated third-party platforms:

- the **Mixpanel** which is popular for its event-level tracking and user flow analysis.
- the **Amplitude** as it is known for robust cohort and retention capabilities.
- and, finally the **Firebase Analytics** which is an easy mobile integration but limited customization.

After proof-of-concept trials, they adopted Mixpanel for its flexible event schema and real-time segmentation, integrating it alongside existing Looker reports to combine deep analysis with executive dashboards.

Overall, building a unified Engagement Metrics Dashboard with integrated feedback loops and specialized analytics tools gave Priya's team a single source of truth. Those insights fueled targeted feature improvements, sharpened stakeholder focus and guided Sakhi toward delivering a truly responsive, user-centered mobile experience.

Balancing Speed with Sensitivity

When Priya Sharma's team saw that if they released a lot of new features too quickly, it could confuse or frustrate users, they realized they needed to take it slow. But, if they were too slow, they might miss out on important improvements. The bi-weekly feedback reviews brought up this tension: power users were happy about the new features, but they said it was hard to adapt to the changes that happened at the same time. Other people were upset about the delayed fixes for important issues. So, the team came up with a plan to deal with these competing demands. They combined real-time backlog adjustments, improved communication protocols, and a thorough sensitivity assessment for each change.

Sensitivity Assessment Framework

When the Sakhi team prepared for upcoming releases, they didn't just look at a feature's RICE score. They also thought about how sensitive each change would be for users, how much it might disrupt daily workflows or affect comfort with the app. In every backlog refinement session, product managers and engineers sat together to give each planned feature a sensitivity score from one to five.

They looked at three things while doing this:

- First, the **scope of impact**, would it be a small, almost invisible UI tweak, or a complete redesign of a core workflow?
- Second, the **user reach**, how many people would feel the change? If it touched a feature that most YUPs used daily, it ranked high.

- And third, the **learning overhead**, would it require users to learn something entirely new, or make them reconsider privacy settings?

Once the sensitivity score was set, they combined it with the RICE score to create a composite priority: RICE divided by Sensitivity. This single number gave them a balanced way to decide what to work on first. High-value features that also carried high sensitivity didn't get rushed, they were given extra preparation, ensuring that when they did arrive, the experience felt smooth and well-thought-out for every user.

Adaptive Backlog Management

Rather than adhere to fixed quarterly plans, the team introduced **flexible backlog sprints**. Every two weeks, stakeholders convened to revisit the composite priorities:

1. Features with **sensitivity ≥4** were split into smaller phases or scheduled in dedicated launch windows with extra user support.
2. Items **scoring 2–3** were batched into grouped releases, reducing cognitive load by limiting context shifts.
3. And, the **quick-win improvements (sensitivity ≤1)** were fast-tracked into hotfix queues, addressing bugs without impacting the broader user experience.

This whole adaptive workflow maintained development momentum while calibrating the user impact of each sprint.

Coordinated Training and Stakeholder Alignment

In addition, recognizing that support and operations teams needed advance notice, the leadership rolled out a **Release Readiness Matrix**:

Change Category	Sensitivity	Communication Channel	Support Training	Executive Briefing
UI Polishes	1–2	Banner + Release Notes	Quick Huddle (15 min)	Weekly Sprint Summary
Workflow Changes	3	Banner + Tour Overlays	Workshop (1 hr)	Bi-Weekly Roadmap Sync
Critical Overhauls	4–5	Email + In-App Guided Tour	Deep-Dive Session (2 hrs)	Pre-Launch Leadership

The support scripts, knowledge-base articles and FAQ updates followed the matrix's guidance. Leadership reviews incorporated sensitivity metrics into sprint retrospectives, fostering transparency across functions.

Continuous Monitoring and Iteration

After the release, we used Sakhi's Engagement Dashboard to get the post-release analytics, and then we fed those straight into the sensitivity recalibration. The team tracked how often the feature was used, how many error reports there were, and the sentiment scores for each release. We made some changes right away to future sensitivity ratings and release strategies because the high-sensitivity features didn't perform well or generated negative feedback. This balanced approach worked well over time. The number of support tickets related to new features dropped by 30%. Overall user satisfaction went up almost half a point on a five-point scale, and the release cycle sped up by 20% without losing clarity or stability.

This case study shows how product managers have to mix user empathy, data-driven frameworks, and adaptive processes to build strong, scalable products. It shows the many skills needed in today's ever-changing development world.

Case-Study Freebies

To accelerate your implementation of Sakhi's persona-driven methodology and Agile practices, leverage the following ready-to-use assets. These templates and frameworks integrate strategic planning, user research and execution guidelines, import them into Miro, Notion, Excel or any collaborative platform.

Detailed Persona Mapping Canvas

Field	Description	Example Data	Notes & Tips
Name	Persona identifier	Young Urban Professional (YUP)	Choose a memorable label that resonates with stakeholders.
Demographics	Age, occupation, location	25–35 yrs, Marketing Manager, Delhi	Add sub-segments (e.g., junior vs. senior-level) for finer granularity.

Device Profile	Smartphone specs, connectivity patterns	Android, 3 GB RAM, 4G + intermittent Wi-Fi	Include preferred OS versions and browser types for web fallback scenarios.
Language Preferences	Primary and secondary languages	English primary; Hindi toggle	Note dialect nuances and formal vs. colloquial usage for copywriting.
Tech Fluency	Comfort with mobile apps and feature complexity	High; uses multiple social and productivity apps daily	Map to support level requirements and tutorial depth.
Pain Points	Key frustrations and unmet needs	Lack of private mentorship forums; unclear event RSVPs	Rank by severity and frequency (e.g., scale of 1–5).
Goals & Motivations	User objectives driving app usage	Career growth; safe community networking	Tie each goal to potential feature outcomes.
Accessibility Needs	Visual, motor or data constraints	Prefers high-contrast UI; offline access required	Specify compliance levels (e.g., WCAG AA).
Acceptance Criteria	Conditions for feature acceptance	Onboarding <2 min; RSVP ≤3 taps	Record how you will measure success (tools, dashboards).

You start by **bringing everyone into the same room**, designers, engineers, product managers, marketers, for a focused **60–90 minute workshop**. This is where the core persona mapping fields get filled out for the first time. People share what they already know from analytics, customer support tickets, and market research, and together you shape those rough insights into a clear, usable profile.

Once you've got that draft, you **take it out into the real world**. You run a handful of short user interviews or send quick follow-up surveys to check whether your assumptions actually match reality. This validation step keeps the persona from being a guess on a slide deck and turns it into something grounded in real user voices.

The work doesn't stop there. **Every quarter**, you revisit the canvas and update it with fresh insights, maybe from new feature launches, shifting user behaviors, or emerging market trends. Over time, the persona evolves alongside your product, staying sharp, accurate, and deeply connected to the people you're building for.

Expanded Cultural Sensitivity & Localization Checklist

Category	Checklist Item	Owner	Frequency	Tool/Resource
Language & Copy	Verify all UI strings in primary and secondary languages; account for tone.	Localization PM	Pre-launch & quarterly	Translation Memory, Glossary
Privacy & Permissions	Confirm opt-in flows for location, notifications and data sharing; audit logs.	UX Lead	Every release	Consent Management Platform
Visual Identity	Review icons, illustrations and color palettes for cultural relevance.	Design Lead	Bi-monthly	Brand Guidelines
Accessibility Compliance	Test UI with screen readers, voice input and adjustable text sizes.	QA Engineer	Every sprint	Axe, Lighthouse

Local Events & Festivities	Incorporate localized imagery and content for major regional events.	Content Lead	Semi-annually	Editorial Calendar
User Feedback Integration	Collect qualitative feedback specifically on cultural fit and tone.	PM Lead	Monthly	UserVoice, In-App Survey Tools

When you're working on new features or updates, you don't just tick off technical tasks, you weave the checklist directly into your **Definition of Done**. That means a ticket isn't considered complete until it passes through every relevant item, from cultural fit to accessibility compliance. It's not an afterthought; it's built into the very fabric of your delivery process.

To make this more than a box-ticking exercise, you **bring in the right voices** at the right time. Cultural consultants help ensure your designs and messaging resonate authentically with the intended audience, avoiding missteps or unintended signals. Accessibility experts, meanwhile, test whether your product truly works for users with different abilities and needs, catching gaps that automated tools or internal teams might miss. The result is a release process that doesn't just deliver features, it delivers them in a way that feels right, works for everyone, and respects the people you're building for.

Comprehensive Workshop Agenda & Facilitation Guide

Time	Activity	Deliverable	Technique/Tool
0–15 min	Welcome & Context Setting	Workshop purpose and success criteria	Slide deck + verbal intro
15–45 min	Persona Deep Dive	Validated persona profiles	Miro board + user quotes

45–75 min	Cultural Mapping	Sensitivity & localization insights	Affinity diagram
75–105 min	Journey Sketching	Key user flows with pain points	Journey map canvas
105–125 min	Prioritization Exercise	Ranked feature backlog with sensitivity scores	Dot voting/MURAL poll
125–140 min	Communication Planning	Release communication draft (banners, tooltips)	Template editing in Notion
140–150 min	Next Steps & Responsibility Assignment	Action items with owners and timelines	Shared task board

A productive session starts long before everyone logs in. You **send out pre-work materials at least 24 hours in advance**, giving participants time to read, reflect, and come prepared with ideas. That way, the actual meeting is about decision-making and collaboration, not catching up. When the session begins, you **split people into virtual breakout rooms** for small-group discussions. This keeps conversations focused, gives quieter voices more space to contribute, and helps generate richer ideas than a single large group often can.

As the session wraps up, you **capture every note, decision, and action item digitally**, no sticky notes lost, no whiteboards erased. Within minutes, the full output is shared with everyone, ensuring clarity, accountability, and momentum for whatever comes next.

Feedback Loop & Sentiment Analysis Framework

Stage	Trigger	Feedback Type	Collection Method	Analysis Metric	Action Pathway

Post-Onboarding	Completion of tutorial	Rating + comment	In-app modal	Tutorial Clarity Score (1–5)	Refine tutorial steps; update tooltips
New Feature Interaction	First use of a major update	Thumbs up/down	Inline prompt	Feature Satisfaction Rate (%)	Adjust UI flows; prioritize bug fixes
Monthly Engagement Checkpoint	Monthly active user login	NPS question	Mini survey	Net Promoter Score	Plan community engagement initiatives
Quarterly Cultural Fit Review	Quarterly user cohort engagement	Open-ended survey	Email + in-app link	Qualitative Themes (coded)	Update localization and content strategies

Instead of waiting for reports to be manually compiled, you **set up automated data pipelines** that feed straight into your analytics dashboards. This gives your team real-time visibility into what's happening, so you can respond to trends or issues the moment they emerge. Every piece of user feedback gets **tagged by persona and region**, adding a layer of context that turns raw comments into actionable insight. You're no longer looking at a vague "user sentiment", you can see exactly how different groups in different places are experiencing the product.

Once a month, the team **comes together for a focused review meeting**. Here, you don't just stare at graphs, you translate insights directly into backlog items. That means real data is shaping the roadmap, ensuring the next sprint tackles the right problems for the right people.

These enriched templates and frameworks empower product teams to operationalize persona insights, cultural sensitivity, collaborative workshops and feedback mechanisms, enabling efficient, inclusive and data-driven product development.

ELEVATING POST-BOOKING AIRLINE SERVICES

This case study looks at SkyLine's strategy to improve the experience for airline passengers after they've booked a ticket. The airline's leadership team came up with a plan for every step of the traveler's journey. They started with booking confirmation and pre-flight communications, and then moved on to check-in, seat assignments, baggage handling, boarding, in-flight services, and arrival support. The exercise revealed hidden frustrations, emotional highs, and system handoffs that often derail seamless travel. They got people from different parts of the company, product, design, engineering, operations, and customer support, to work together to turn qualitative anecdotes and quantitative data into a visual journey mural. We focused on the most important issues and made improvements to services like baggage policies, seat recommendations, and notifications. It'll teach you how to run an immersive journey-mapping workshop, spot the points where things get in the way, and turn those insights into real-world prototypes.

Customer Journey Mapping Workshop

A week into planning SkyLine's post-booking enhancements, the airline called for a comprehensive journey-mapping workshop. Participants spanned product, engineering, design, operations and customer service, reflecting the cross-functional effort required to improve every passenger interaction after booking. The airline began by presenting synthesized user data, survey results from 2,000 recent flyers, transcripts of 300 support calls and usage analytics showing drop-off hotspots. She then sketched a horizontal timeline, dividing the post-booking experience into seven critical stages:

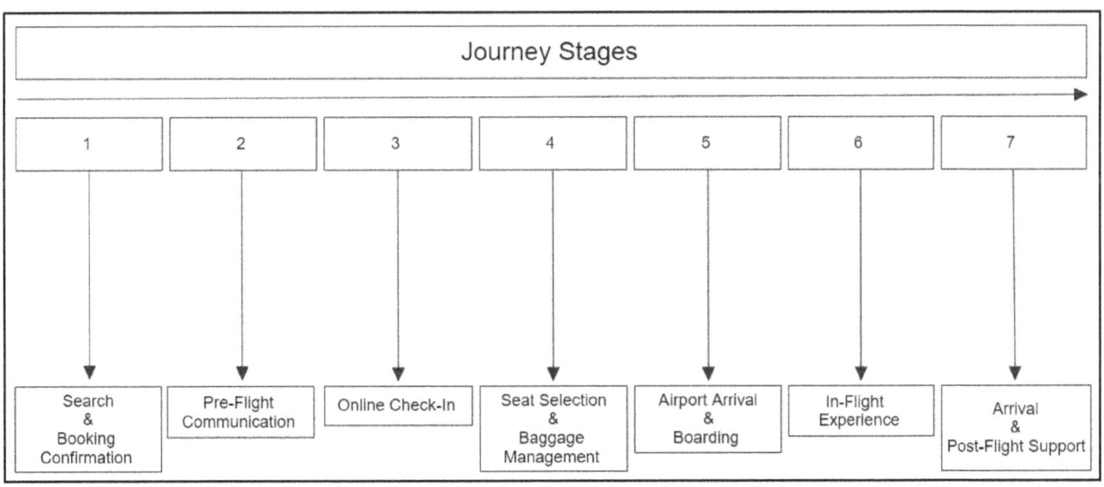

Fig 3.1 Post-Booking Experience Timeline

1. Search & Booking Confirmation
2. Pre-Flight Communication
3. Online Check-In
4. Seat Selection & Baggage Management
5. Airport Arrival & Boarding
6. In-Flight Experience
7. Arrival & Post-Flight Support

Search & Booking Confirmation

First, the group started mapping the moment a passenger confirmed a booking. The yellow sticky notes showed excitement about discounted fares and loyalty rewards, while the red ones highlighted confusion about change policies. The facilitators encouraged team members to write down their emotions ("relief," "uncertainty") and the systems they used, email notifications, mobile push messages, and SMS alerts.

Here are some of the main points from the meeting:

- Promotional emails often ended up in spam folders, which delayed confirmation.
- Hey, just a heads-up: the change-request links are redirecting to outdated webpages, which is causing errors.
- Messaging that lacked personalization left frequent flyers in the dark about their tier benefits.

Pre-Flight Communication

During this stage, the participants mapped touchpoints, such as notification of gate assignments, weather alerts and itinerary reminders. And, the following pain points emerged:

- Unclear visa reminders led to last-minute support calls.
- Inconsistent email formatting obscured lounge access information.

Post this, the teams drafted solutions on green notes, such as rule-based SMS digests and agent-reviewed pre-flight checklists.

Online Check-In

During online check-in, this phase revealed both delight and frustration. Green notes said how easy mobile check-in is, while red notes showed concern about hidden baggage fees.

Some of the underlying issues were:

- Mobile check-in forms lacked clear baggage-allowance calculators.
- Frequent travelers reported inconsistent recognition of elite status, preventing priority check-in.

At the workshop, designers came up with an online baggage calculator and VIP badge overlay.

Seat Selection & Baggage Management

On the whiteboard, there were sketches of layouts for the seating maps. The attendees highlighted sticky clusters where families struggled to get seats next to each other and business travelers had to pay a lot for upgrades. We also found some problems with the baggage management system.

They are:

- Weight limits varied by fare class but weren't highlighted.
- Oversized carry-on rules differed internationally, causing gate-side disputes.

The participants suggested dynamic seat recommendations for groups and real-time baggage-fee estimations integrated into the seat-selection flow. seat recommendations for groups and real-time baggage-fee estimations integrated into the seat-selection flow.

Airport Arrival & Boarding

When it came to getting to the airport and getting on the plane, this stage showed just how complicated handoffs can be. Operations leads imagined baggage check-in kiosks, while support reps added customer anecdotes of long lines.

Following are the main points of contention:

- Automated kiosks rejected boarding passes if minor name mismatches occurred, leading to gate delays.
- Lack of digital wayfinding meant passengers missed gates in large terminals.

The green-inked solutions they came up with included mobile map integration and AI-driven name-matching tolerance during kiosk scans.

In-Flight Experience

When we were flying, we got a mix of views from different people involved. The flight attendants talked about the problems with the logistics, and the passengers' virtual representations on the map showed that they wanted to know the flight status right away.

Following are some of the main problems they identified:

- Meal preferences logged during booking were lost onboard.
- No mid-flight notifications for connecting flight gate changes.

The team brainstormed end-to-end data sync with crew tablets and personalized in-flight communication channels.

Arrival & Post-Flight Support

When they landed, passengers looked for baggage-claim notifications and ride-sharing integrations. Sticky notes showed you which alerts you missed and which numbers on the baggage carousel were confusing. What we learned is:

- International travelers lacked clarity on customs procedures.
- Families struggled coordinating rides for multiple passengers and luggage.

The teams sketched a unified post-flight dashboard: live baggage tracking, customs tips and partnered ride-options, all in the app. a unified post-flight dashboard: live baggage tracking, customs tips and partnered ride-options, all in the app.

With seven stages fully annotated, the workshop shifted to drawing arrows between related pain points. The support ticket clusters guided attention to critical hand-off systems: notification dispatch, booking APIs and baggage management databases. The group used dot-voting (each member had five votes) to indicate highest-impact areas. And, the top priorities emerged as below:

1. Seat selection refinements for groups.
2. Baggage allowance clarity within check-in.
3. Real-time baggage tracking post-landing.

In response, the cross-functional pods formed instantly, each tasked with rapid prototyping and user-testing these improvements. By the day's end, following artifacts were included:

- A large, color-coded journey mural.
- A ranked backlog of twelve service enhancements.
- Prototype sketches, wireframes and API flow diagrams.

The facilitators scheduled follow-up user interviews and assigned owners to each improvement pod. This workshop was key to setting up Skyline's integration sprints, making sure that product decisions were based on what passengers want.

System Integration Plan

After the customer journey mapping workshop, the airline's engineering and product teams got together to create a complete integration plan that would connect modern microservices with the company's older reservation systems. This plan included API contracts for critical features like real-time PNR (Passenger Name Record) status, baggage tracking, managing ancillary services, and delivering notifications. It also had clear SLA targets and rollback protocols to make sure the system was reliable.

Core Integrations

The team identified four primary integration touchpoints:

1. **PNR Status Service**

   This handles the heartbeat of the booking journey. It keeps passengers updated with real-time booking confirmations, notifies them instantly of itinerary changes, and ensures they have the latest seat assignments.

2. **Baggage Tracking Service**

   Built for transparency and reassurance, this service monitors checked luggage at every critical point: departure, transfer, and arrival. Each scan event is fed back to the user so they always know exactly where their bags are.

3. **Ancillary Services Service**

   Beyond the ticket itself, this system manages all the extras that elevate the journey, adding extra baggage allowance, selecting meals, booking lounge access, or enabling priority boarding.

4. **Notification Service**

   The communication hub. It sends email, SMS, and in-app push notifications to keep passengers informed of updates, reminders, and urgent alerts, ensuring no message is missed.

To meet different operational needs, **every touchpoint supported both asynchronous event-driven updates** (for instant pushes like a gate change) **and synchronous query endpoints** (for on-demand checks like confirming baggage status). This dual approach balanced **speed, reliability, and control**, ensuring passengers received timely, accurate information no matter when or how they accessed it.

Sample API Contracts

The integration plan documented RESTful endpoints with sample request and response schemas, accompanied by OpenAPI specification snippets.

```
openapi: 3.0.1
info:
  title: SkyLine PNR Status API
  version: '1.0'
paths:
  /pnr/{pnrNumber}/status:
    get:
      summary: Retrieve PNR status details
      parameters:
        - in: path
          name: pnrNumber
          required: true
          schema:
            type: string
          description: The PNR identifier
      responses:
        '200':
          description: PNR status payload
          content:
            application/json:
              schema:
                type: object
                properties:
                  pnrNumber:
                    type: string
                  status:
                    type: string
```

```
segments:
  type: array
  items:
    type: object
    properties:
      flightNumber:
        type: string
      departureTime:
        type: string
        format: date-time
      arrivalTime:
        type: string
        format: date-time
```


And for baggage, the team defined a WebSocket-based event stream to deliver scan updates in real time:


```
{
  "eventType": "BAGGAGE_SCAN",
  "timestamp": "2025-08-01T14:32:00Z",
  "bagTag": "ABC123",
  "location": "JFK-BHS-COUNT"
}
```


SLA Targets and Performance Requirements

To ensure high availability and responsiveness, the integration SLAs were established:

Endpoint	99.9th Percentile Latency	Uptime Target	Error Budget (per month)
GET /pnr/{pnr}/status	≤200 ms	99.95%	22 minutes

WebSocket Baggage Stream	≤500 ms	99.9%	43 minutes
POST /ancillary/{pnr}/add	≤300 ms	99.9%	43 minutes
POST /notifications/send	≤250 ms	99.9%	43 minutes

The SLO monitoring dashboards, powered by Prometheus and Grafana, would track these metrics, triggering alerts when error budgets were consumed above thresholds.

Rollback Strategies

Given the criticality of reservation data, the plan incorporated layered rollback methods:

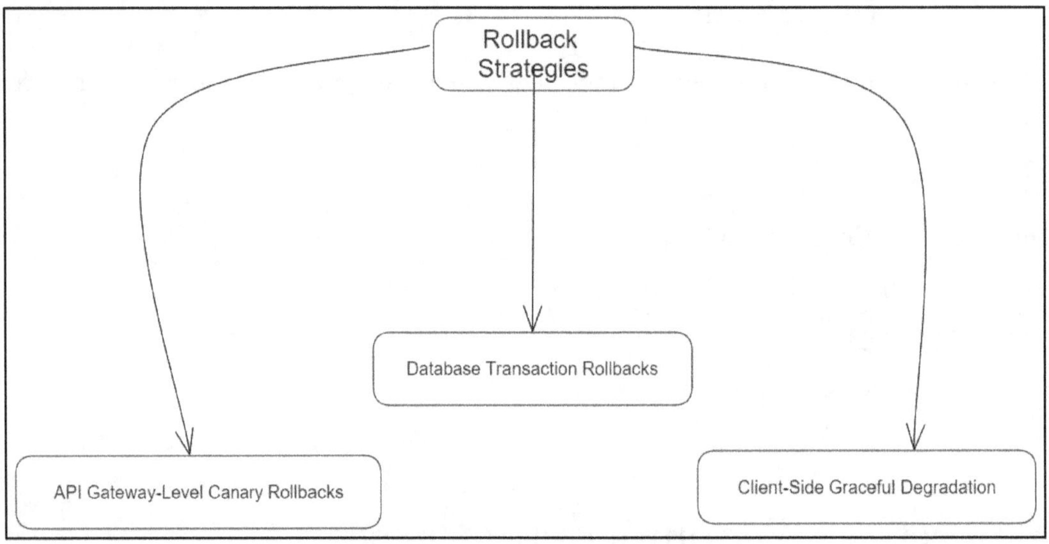

Fig 3.2 Rollback Strategies

API Gateway-Level Canary Rollbacks

Every new deployment began with a **90/10 traffic split**, 90% of traffic went to the stable version, and 10% to the new release. This small-scale exposure allowed the system to monitor for anomalies in real-time. If metrics flagged errors, latency spikes, or abnormal patterns, the system automatically routed all traffic back to the last stable build. This safeguarded passengers from widespread impact while allowing fast detection of deployment issues.

Database Transaction Rollbacks

Schema changes and data migrations carried the risk of breaking compatibility. To manage this, feature flags controlled migration scripts, enabling immediate disablement if problems emerged. By keeping the old schema accessible, the team could instantly reverse incompatible changes without corrupting reservation data, preserving business continuity.

Client-Side Graceful Degradation

Even if APIs failed completely, the **mobile app remained functional** for passengers. Cached **PNR snapshots** allowed users to see their latest booking details offline. A retry option encouraged reconnection when service was restored. This meant that passengers never felt "locked out" of essential travel info, even in the middle of an outage.

When you put these three layers together, the rollback system can respond in minutes, which minimizes any disruptions, keeps your data intact, and makes sure passengers can still access the info they need, all of which is super important in a high-pressure travel situation.

Legacy System Interoperability

The reservation engine at SkyLine, which was built on a monolithic COBOL-based mainframe, exposed limited SOAP endpoints for PNR reads and writes. The integration plan said to use an adapter microservice to translate REST calls to SOAP messages, encapsulating legacy quirks while presenting clean JSON interfaces to downstream services.

Below is a sample adapter logic in pseudo-code:

```
public PnrStatus getPnrStatus(String pnr) {
    SoapClient soap = new SoapClient(legacyEndpoint);
    PnrResponse response = soap.call("GetPnrStatus", new PnrRequest(pnr));
    return mapToPnrStatus(response);
}
```

The team was able to cut down on the changes needed for the old system and kept the complexities in one place by taking out this adapter layer.

Testing and Validation

To ensure integrations were **fully functional from one end to the other**, the team built a multi-layered validation mechanism that caught issues before they could reach passengers.

Contract Testing with Pact

Here, **consumer-driven tests** checked whether the client's expectations matched the actual behavior of the provider's API. This meant every data format, response field, and interaction was verified before integration went live, ensuring no surprises during deployment. It was like a pre-flight checklist for system compatibility.

Sandbox Environments

A **mirrored instance of the legacy reservation system** acted as a safe playground for experiments. Teams could run high-risk scenarios, try new features, and simulate failures without touching live passenger data. This allowed realistic, hands-on testing without fear of disrupting real bookings.

Synthetic Monitoring Probes

Even after integrations passed testing, **automated scripts ran every five minutes**, calling each endpoint to verify both **response schemas** and **performance baselines**. If something slowed down or broke unexpectedly, alerts went out immediately, keeping the team proactive rather than reactive.

They combined pre-deployment verification, safe experimentation, and continuous real-time checks. This strategy gave the team confidence that integrations would work not just once, but even under the pressures of real-world usage.

Iterative Rollout Plan

After that, they moved on to the deployments, which followed a phased model.

Internal Beta

Only 10% of the staff are doing that, and they're checking the user interface and the backend interactions.

Soft Launch

We've released it to 5% of real users with non-critical bookings.

Full Rollout

We'll be rolling it out over the next week, keeping an eye on it all the time against our SLA dashboards.

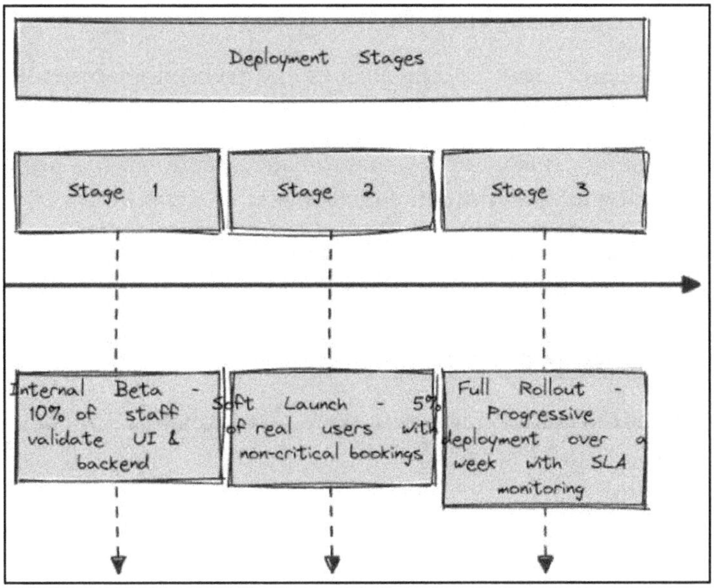

Fig 3.3 Phased Deployment Plan

The feedback loops between operations and product teams captured issues in a shared incident tracker, ensuring rapid remediation.

Service-Level Negotiation Script

One morning, the SkyLine team was surprised to find a sudden surge in incident reports. It turned out that delays in baggage-tracking and PNR mismatches had led to a spike in customer complaints overnight. The airline's leaders realized that their usual informal ways of dealing with these issues wouldn't be enough, so they got together for a quick meeting. They didn't have any kind of plan for formal SLAs, and the pressure of handling more and more support requests made them think seriously about commitments. That urgency led to a negotiation script with a structure, which was created as a role-play exercise to make sure everyone was on the same page about response times, error budgets, and clear escalation paths. The team used precise language patterns, win–win framing, and stakeholder cues to create an impromptu framework.

Negotiation Prep

Before entering any discussion, the negotiation team gathered data to support its position. They compiled:

- Charts showing current incident response times and uptime percentages for core services (PNR status updates, baggage-tracking events, notification delivery).
- Concrete examples from the journey-mapping workshop illustrating passenger

frustration points caused by slow system responses.

- Industry SLA standards from leading airlines and technology providers, establishing a baseline for realistic targets.
- An outline of existing capacity limits, maintenance windows and peak-load expectations, transparently acknowledging potential challenges.

When you've got these materials ready, the negotiation script gets everyone on the same page for working together instead of fighting.

Script Structure and Key Phases

The service-level negotiation script unfolded over three phases: Opening, Exploration, and Agreement. Each phase featured scripted dialogue prompts, expected partner responses and suggested follow-up questions.

Opening Phase

The goal is to start on the right foot, set a friendly tone, agree on the objectives, and make sure both sides know what success looks like.

Moderator: "Thank you for joining us today. Our shared objective is to ensure that our passengers receive seamless updates, from booking changes to baggage tracking, without encountering frustrating delays. We value your partnership and want to align on realistic, measurable commitments that benefit both parties."

Vendor Response Cue: "We appreciate SkyLine's commitment to passenger experience. Our team is dedicated to delivering timely updates and we look forward to collaborating on SLA targets."

Follow-Up Prompt: "To start, could you walk us through your current standard response times and how you handle peak-load scenarios?"

Exploration Phase

This part's about the nitty-gritty: what's technically possible, where things get tricky, and what changes might be needed.

Moderator: "Our data shows that 90th percentile latency for PNR status queries currently sits at 350 ms, but delays above 200 ms correlate with increased support calls. We propose targeting 200 ms at the 95th percentile. Could you share the feasibility of that metric based on your system architecture?"

Vendor Response Cue: "Achieving 200 ms consistently will require adjustments. During peak times, we see spikes up to 500 ms. We could invest in additional caching layers or scale-out strategies to narrow the gap."

Follow-Up Prompt: "Understood. What effort and timeline would you estimate for implementing such optimizations, and how might we phase the rollout to minimize risk?”

Moderator: “Regarding baggage-tracking events, we’d like scan updates to propagate within 500 ms of each event. Currently, variance in location services leads to occasional delays up to 2 seconds. How can we reduce that variance?”

Vendor Response Cue: “By refining message queue priorities and optimizing WebSocket throughput, we can aim for under 750 ms in the next quarter, then work toward 500 ms in six months.”

Follow-Up Prompt: “That phased model makes sense. Let’s document interim targets and reassess at each milestone.”

Agreement Phase

Here, you lock in the targets, escalation procedures, and how progress will be reviewed.

Moderator: “To summarize, we agree on the following:

- PNR status queries: 95th percentile latency ≤200 ms by Q2.
- Baggage events: average propagation ≤750 ms by end of Q1, improving to ≤500 ms by Q3.
- Notification delivery: 99.9% success within 250 ms.
- Shall we formalize these in a joint SLA addendum?”

Vendor Response Cue: “Yes, those metrics reflect a balanced target. We will draft the SLA addendum and include escalation contacts.”

Moderator: “Excellent. Let’s also define escalation paths:

- Tier-1: Automated alert to on-call engineer within 5 minutes of breach detection.
- Tier-2: Daily review with operations manager if error budget exceeds 10%.
- Tier-3: Executive review if error budget breaches 25% in a rolling month.
- We’ll schedule monthly SLA review meetings to track progress. Does that align with your internal processes?”

Vendor Response Cue: “Absolutely. Those tiers match our standard incident-management workflows.”

Throughout the script, the negotiators used phrases like "we propose," "together we can," and "our shared objective" to foster partnership. They didn't give ultimatums, and instead talked about what was good for both sides. For example, they said that improving latency by 150 milliseconds would reduce support call volume by 20%, which would free up both teams to work on other important things. They also said that they understand how complicated real-time messaging can be during busy times, and that they appreciate the team's work to make the queue processing better.

And by talking about technical targets in terms of business impact and shared value, the script kept moving forward and building trust.

Drafting SLA Addendum

As soon as they reached an agreement, the airline's legal and vendor-management teams wrote an SLA addendum that included:

- Precise descriptions of each KPI, calculation methods and data sources.
- Monthly performance reviews, quarterly business reviews and annual contract renewals.
- Contact hierarchies, response windows and resolution timelines.
- Error-budget overages triggered credit back to the airline; consistent overperformance earned vendor bonuses.

The last step was to plan a formal sign-off meeting, hand out the SLA document, and update the internal dashboards. Automated alerts were set up to track SLA adherence in real time, and stakeholders got weekly reports that gave a summary of performance metrics.

This service-level negotiation script is pretty extensive. It's based on role-play, data-backed proposals, and collaborative language. It made sure that SkyLine secured realistic, measurable commitments from its operations and vendor partners. These commitments are key to the elevated post-booking services that are central to passenger satisfaction.

Kanban Process Flow Configuration

The airline's post-booking enhancements depended on an operational framework capable of handling diverse requests without delays. When product, support and engineering teams reviewed ticket backlogs, they found that sprint rhythms and ad-hoc handoffs frequently stalled urgent fixes and feature work. To address these challenges, the leadership team designed a two-lane Kanban board that directly linked customer-support tickets to engineering tasks, ensuring a transparent, end-to-end workflow.

In the **Support-to-Dev** Lane, incoming issues, ranging from baggage inquiries to seat-assignment requests, flowed through initial triage, where impact and urgency were assessed. Color-coded cards denoted ticket type and severity, allowing support leads to categorize incidents quickly. Once classified, high-priority tickets advanced to the "Ready for Dev" column, complete with annotated reproduction steps and user context.

Meanwhile, the **Engineering Implementation** Lane housed the development pipeline for backlog items. Engineers pulled cards marked Ready for Dev into the "To Do" column, then moved them through "In Progress," "Code Review," "QA Testing" and "Done." Each stage carried explicit entry and exit criteria, displayed on the board to eliminate guesswork. The entire board served as a single source of truth: support could monitor progress, and engineering retained the customer context necessary to deliver effective solutions.

A critical aspect of this Kanban configuration was the strict enforcement of Work-In-Progress (WIP) limits. The team capped the number of tickets in triage and active development, preventing overloading and encouraging rapid throughput. Clear swimlanes segmented critical production issues, planned enhancements and technical debt, ensuring that urgent matters never drowned in routine tasks. Together, these elements reduced cycle times, eliminated handoff confusion and created a continuous delivery engine that kept pace with passenger needs.

Designing Two-Lane Structure

The configuration revolved around two main workflow lanes, each with a distinct purpose but connected in how they moved work forward.

The **Support-to-Dev Queue** was owned by the Customer Support team. This lane acted as the bridge between user problems and engineering action. It started with *New Tickets*, moved into *Triage In Progress*, and ended at *Ready for Dev*. Here, a triage engineer reviewed each ticket logged by front-line agents, checking its severity, how many users it affected, and whether it could be reproduced. Once sorted, the most urgent bugs and valuable feature requests were turned into detailed user stories, complete with acceptance criteria and links back to the original ticket for context.

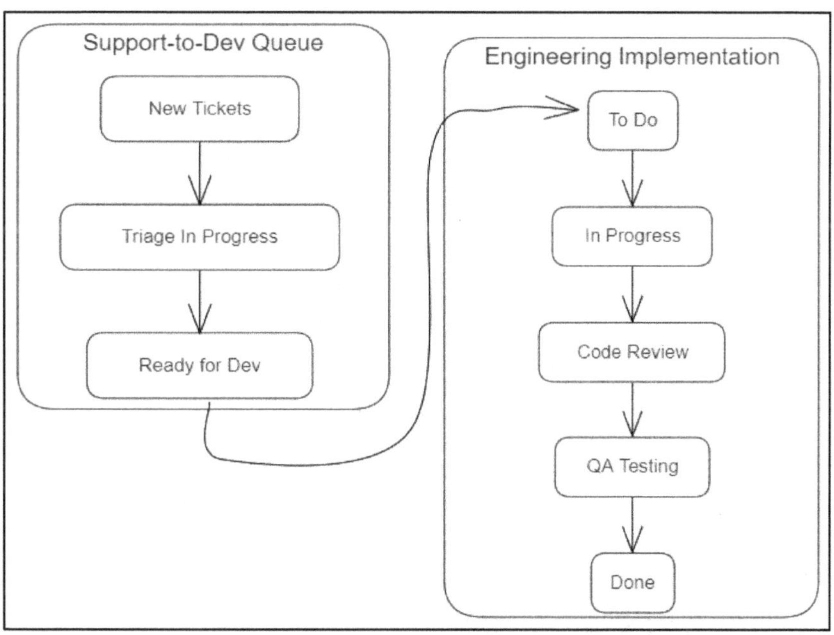

Fig 3.4 Two-Lane Structure Design

From there, these stories entered the **Engineering Implementation** Lane, owned by the Development team. This was where ideas became real, production-ready features. The workflow here progressed from *To Do*, to *In Progress*, then *Code Review*, *QA Testing*, and finally *Done.*

Every ticket or story card traveled this journey, from a user's initial problem report, through careful triage, to the engineering team's delivery of a tested, working solution. It ensured nothing got lost in translation and that every change was grounded in real user needs.

Implementing WIP Limits

To maintain focus and reduce context switching, the team imposed WIP limits on key columns:

	WIP Limit	Rationale
Triage In Progress	5	Prevent backlog choke; ensure swift evaluation
In Progress	3 per engineer	Avoid parallel task overload
QA Testing	4	Balance test load with availability

These limits popped up as visual cues on the digital board. When a column reached capacity, team members paused new work until cards advanced downstream.

Crafting "Done" Criteria

When it wasn't clear what "finished" really meant, work often got sent back to earlier stages, wasting time and creating frustration. To fix this, the team agreed on specific **"Done" criteria** for each stage of the workflow as shown below:

- For **Code Review to QA Testing**, a pull request had to be approved by two peers, the automated build had to pass, and unit test coverage needed to be at least 85%.
- For **QA Testing to Done**, all manual test cases had to be completed, the regression suite had to pass, and performance metrics had to meet the agreed service levels.
- For **Support-to-Dev Ready for Dev**, tickets needed to be properly categorized, include details on user impact, and provide clear reproduction steps.

These rules were built right into the card templates so everyone, from support triage to developers, knew exactly what was required before moving work forward. They also powered automated checks in the CI/CD pipeline, blocking any code merges or deployments that didn't meet the standards.

Metrics and Monitoring

To see how well their Kanban process was working, the team kept a close eye on a few key metrics, including the following:

- **Cycle Time** measured how long it took, on average, for a card to travel from *Ready for Dev* to *Done.*
- **Lead Time** looked at the bigger picture, tracking the total time from when a support ticket was first created to when the related feature was fully deployed.
- **Throughput** counted how many cards were completed each week, giving a snapshot of delivery speed.
- **Blocked Time** showed the total number of hours cards spent stuck in a *Blocked* status, helping the team pinpoint bottlenecks that slowed progress.

The dashboards displayed rolling four-week averages. A consistent rise in cycle time triggered retrospective action items, such as rebalancing WIP limits or clarifying acceptance criteria. However, despite robust planning, urgent production incidents occasionally surfaced. The Kanban configuration incorporated an **Escalation Lane** for rapid-response cards:

- Any card flagged "Escalation" by support automatically bypassed WIP limits in the Critical Production Issues swimlane.
- A dedicated on-call engineer pulled the top escalation card within 15 minutes, conducting a triage call and assigning a fix priority.
- Post-resolution, the card re-entered the normal workflow for root-cause analysis and permanent remedy.

This mechanism balanced stability with agility, ensuring customer-impacting issues received immediate attention without derailing the broader sprint. This whole Kanban process flow configuration became the operational backbone for SkyLine's post-booking innovation, reducing friction between support and development while maintaining a culture of continuous delivery and customer-centric responsiveness.

Support Metrics Tracker Queries

When the airline saw a sudden jump in unresolved support tickets that showed gaps in visibility, the analytics team knew they needed a toolkit for on-the-spot reporting. They quickly put together a set of ready-to-go SQL snippets to track important support metrics like Average Resolution Time, First-Contact Resolution Rate, and Repeat-Contact Ratio, by pulling directly from customer-support and engineering tables. When we put these searches into real-time dashboards, we turned raw data into useful info, giving teams clear answers right away about adherence to service level agreements. With this info, stakeholders can spot bottlenecks, tweak processes, and deal with issues before they affect passenger satisfaction.

Average Resolution Time (ART)

This is meant to measure the mean time elapsed from ticket creation to resolution, highlighting overall speed of support operations. To figure out this metric, simply consider to have the following tables ready:

- **support_tickets(ticket_id, created_at, resolved_at**, and
- **ticket_status(status, ticket_id, status_timestamp)**

And then, run the following queries:

```
-- Calculate average resolution time in hours for the past 30 days
SELECT
  DATE_TRUNC('day', st.created_at) AS day,
  AVG(EXTRACT(epoch FROM (st.resolved_at - st.created_at)) / 3600) AS
avg_resolution_hours
FROM support_tickets st
WHERE st.resolved_at IS NOT NULL
  AND st.created_at >= CURRENT_DATE - INTERVAL '30 days'
GROUP BY DATE_TRUNC('day', st.created_at)
ORDER BY day;
```

Here, the **EXTRACT(epoch FROM ...) / 3600** converts the resolution interval into hours. The grouping by day surfaces daily trends, thereby helping us the detection of weekly patterns (e.g., slower weekends).

First-Contact Resolution Rate (FCR)

This metric is meant to determine the percentage of tickets resolved without further follow-up, reflecting support efficiency and knowledge completeness. To figure out this metric, simply consider to have the following tables ready:

- Support_tickets, and
- ticket_interactions(interaction_id, ticket_id)

And then, run the following queries:

```
-- Calculate first-contact resolution rate over the past month
```

```
WITH first_interactions AS (
  SELECT ticket_id, MIN(interaction_timestamp) AS first_ts
  FROM ticket_interactions
  GROUP BY ticket_id
),
resolution_counts AS (
  SELECT
    t.ticket_id,
    CASE WHEN t.resolved_at <= fi.first_ts THEN 1 ELSE 0 END AS resolved_first_contact
  FROM support_tickets t
  JOIN first_interactions fi ON t.ticket_id = fi.ticket_id
  WHERE t.created_at >= CURRENT_DATE - INTERVAL '30 days'
)
SELECT
  ROUND(100.0 * SUM(resolved_first_contact) / COUNT(*), 2) AS fcr_percentage
FROM resolution_counts;
```

Here, the CTE **first_interactions** captures the timestamp of the first agent response. The tickets resolved at or before that timestamp count toward FCR. And, the percentage calculation yields a daily or rolling FCR if desired.

Repeat-Contact Ratio (RCR)

This is meant to quantify the proportion of tickets requiring multiple touches, indicating unresolved issues or process gaps. To figure out this metric, simply consider to have the following tables ready:

- support_tickets, and
- ticket_interactions

And then, run the following queries:

```
-- Compute repeat-contact ratio for the last 30 days
WITH interaction_counts AS (
  SELECT ticket_id, COUNT(*) AS interaction_count
```

```
  FROM ticket_interactions
  GROUP BY ticket_id
)
SELECT
  ROUND(100.0 * SUM(CASE WHEN ic.interaction_count > 1 THEN 1 ELSE 0 END) / COUNT(*), 2) AS rcr_percentage
FROM interaction_counts ic
JOIN support_tickets st ON ic.ticket_id = st.ticket_id
WHERE st.created_at >= CURRENT_DATE - INTERVAL '30 days';
```

Here, the tickets with more than one interaction indicate repeat contacts. The High RCR suggests root-cause fixes or knowledge-base improvements may be required.

Below is a sample code of how the team embedded these SQL queries into a Python script for automated reporting:

```
import psycopg2
import pandas as pd
def fetch_metric(sql_query):
    conn = psycopg2.connect(dbname='support_db', user='analyst', password='***')
    df = pd.read_sql(sql_query, conn)
    conn.close()
    return df
# Fetch ART
art_query = """<Average Resolution Time SQL>"""
art_df = fetch_metric(art_query)
# Fetch FCR
fcr_query = """<First Contact Resolution SQL>"""
fcr_df = fetch_metric(fcr_query)
# Combine and send report
report_df = art_df.merge(fcr_df, on='day')
report_df.to_csv('weekly_support_metrics.csv', index=False)
```

This script was set to run on a Monday morning cron job, sending the CSV to stakeholders and updating the BI dataset API. With these support metrics tracker queries, the SkyLine created a solid, data-driven foundation for making sure they're always meeting the service levels that passengers expect.

Streamlining Hand-Offs

But when the post-booking initiatives kept missing delivery windows, the airline's leaders realized that the issue was actually due to some hand-off problems. There were a ton of support tickets in triage, and developers were waiting for deployment approvals, so delivery took hours and hours. To deal with this, a team made up of support leads, software engineers, and data analysts got together to figure out what was causing the delays and how to stop them.

Mapping Every Handoff

During a collaborative whiteboard session, the team walked through the entire path of a high-priority support ticket, step by step.

It began with **Triage Completion**, where support marked a ticket as *Ready for Dev* after the initial assessment. From there, **Engineering Pickup** happened when a developer claimed the ticket and moved it into active development. Once the work was complete, it entered **Code Review**, awaiting peer approval. Finally, the **Deployment** stage merged the approved code into the main branch and pushed it live to production.

Timestamps told an important story: on average, there were **18 hours** between triage and development start, **12 hours** spent in code review, and **20 hours** before deployment. These delays grew even longer over weekends and off-peak hours, leaving urgent tickets idle for far too long.

Root-Cause Analysis

The data-driven retrospectives revealed three main culprits:

- First is that the triage engineers had to manually create and assign Jira stories, leading to batch handoffs and uneven attention.
- The second is that the strict release calendar allowed just two deployments per day, slowing urgent fixes.
- And, the last is that without real-time alerts, the developers often didn't realize a ticket had landed on their plate.

Automation Blueprint

To eliminate these bottlenecks, the team designed three automation initiatives:

1. **Automatic Ticket Conversion**
2. **On-Merge Deployment Triggers**
3. **Immediate Assignment Notifications**

To anchor their efforts, the task force set explicit quarterly goals:

Metric	Baseline	Target	Deadline
Triage-to-Dev Lead Time	18 hrs	≤6 hrs	Q4 End
Review-to-Deploy Lead Time	20 hrs	≤8 hrs	Q4 End
Automation Coverage	0%	100%	Q4 Midpoint

The dashboards surfaced these metrics in real time, driven by SQL queries and telemetry from the Kanban board and CI/CD system. The alerts notified the team when any metric deviated beyond a 20% error budget, triggering immediate remediation sprints.

Within eight weeks of full rollout:

- **Triage-to-Dev Lead Time** fell by 70% to 5.4 hours.
- **Review-to-Deploy Lead Time** dropped by 60% to 8 hours.
- **Support Satisfaction** scores rose by 15% as critical issues reached resolution faster.

By the end of that intensive eight-week effort, the SkyLine achieved its automation and lead-time reduction goals ahead of schedule. Triage-to-Dev lead time shrank from 18 hours to just 5 hours, and Review-to-Deploy time fell from 20 to 8 hours. Support satisfaction scores climbed by 15%, and customer ticket backlog dropped by 70%. This transformation demonstrated how precise measurement, targeted automation and cross-team collaboration can redefine operational efficiency. In just two months, the SkyLine not only met its targets but also established a durable foundation for ongoing innovation wherein the data-driven processes elevate service quality in the fast-paced airline industry.

Case-Study Freebies

Following is a service gap mapping model that helped SkyLine make some major changes after their booking system was set up. Add it to your workshop toolkit and tweak it to fit your needs.

Stage	Customer Goal	Pain Point	Backend System	Improvement Idea
Booking Confirmation	Verify booking details	Confusing change links	Reservation API	Inline change-policy calculator
Online Check-In	Complete check-in quickly	Unclear baggage allowances	Check-In Service	Embedded baggage-fee calculator
Seat Selection & Baggage Mgmt	Choose seats and manage luggage easily	Seats not held together for groups	Seat-Management Microservice	Smart-group seat recommendations
Boarding	Arrive at gate on time	Kiosk rejects minor name mismatches	Boarding Pass System	AI-tolerant name-matching logic
In-Flight Communication	Access flight updates and services	Lost meal and connection notifications	Crew Tablet Integration	Real-time sync with passenger profiles
Arrival & Baggage Delivery	Retrieve luggage without delay	Missing carousel alerts	Baggage Tracking Event Stream	Push notifications with live tracking

This grid is essentially a problem-solving map that connects each stage of the passenger journey to its goal, pain points, the backend system responsible, and a practical improvement idea. It's designed to pinpoint where the customer experience breaks down and match those gaps with actionable fixes.

ONBOARDING NEW DEVELOPERS TO CODE PLATFORM

For years, the CodeHub has been the go-to for collaborative software development at businesses all around the world. Teams count on its integrated CI/CD pipelines, in-browser code editing, advanced search features, and detailed permission controls to deliver top-notch features at scale. But there was a problem beneath the surface. New users, especially external contractors and junior team members, had a hard time finishing even basic onboarding tasks. Our internal analytics showed that while marketing campaigns and user outreach drove sign-ups, fewer than one-third of those accounts ever reached the critical "repository clone" stage. Of those, less than half went on to make a first commit, and only 15% submitted an initial pull request in their first week. The fact that so many people were signing up and then dropping out put a damper on the company's ability to achieve its long-term goals. Not only that, but it also led to higher support costs and made the company look bad to developers who might've otherwise used it.

When we interviewed new CodeHub users, we found that there were some common problems. The instructions to set it up were really long and hard to understand. It had a lot of commands in the terminal, and the documentation was all over the place, spread out on different wikis. There wasn't any clear guidance in the app, so a lot of people ended up searching for help on other forums or just left the platform. The leadership team knew that first impressions are key, and they wanted to make sure that new developers felt welcome and supported right from the start. So, they decided to give the onboarding process a thorough makeover. They came up with a main goal: get the number of new users reaching their first pull request up from 15% to 50% over the next quarter.

To get there, product, engineering, and UX specialists worked together on a multi-stage approach:

- Use drop-off funnel analysis to figure out exactly where people are dropping off.
- API & Documentation Playbook to consolidate and contextualize developer references.
- Setting up an Experimentation Framework to safely test iterative improvements.
- The Mentorship Rotation Model will provide real-time guidance.
- The time-to-first-pull-request metric is a way to track progress and see if you're on track to meet your goals.

This chapter dives deeply into the first initiative, **Drop-Off Funnel Analysis**, detailing how instrumentation, quantitative and qualitative diagnostics and targeted flow redesigns led to a dramatic uplift in onboarding completion rates.

Drop-Off Funnel Analysis

Developer Onboarding Funnel

To figure out exactly where new developers were dropping out of the onboarding process, the team mapped the journey into six clear stages, each representing a major milestone on CodeHub.

- It all begins with **Account Activation**, where a new user signs up and verifies their email.
- Once inside, they move to **Dashboard Exploration**, taking their first look around the CodeHub interface.
- From there, they hit **Repository Discovery**, where they click into a sample repository to explore its contents. The next step, **Repository Cloning**, is when they run a git clone command, either through the embedded IDE or their own terminal, to start working locally.
- Once they have the code, they progress to **First Local Commit**, making and saving their first change on their machine.
- Finally comes the big moment: **First Pull Request Submission**, where they send their changes back to the main branch.

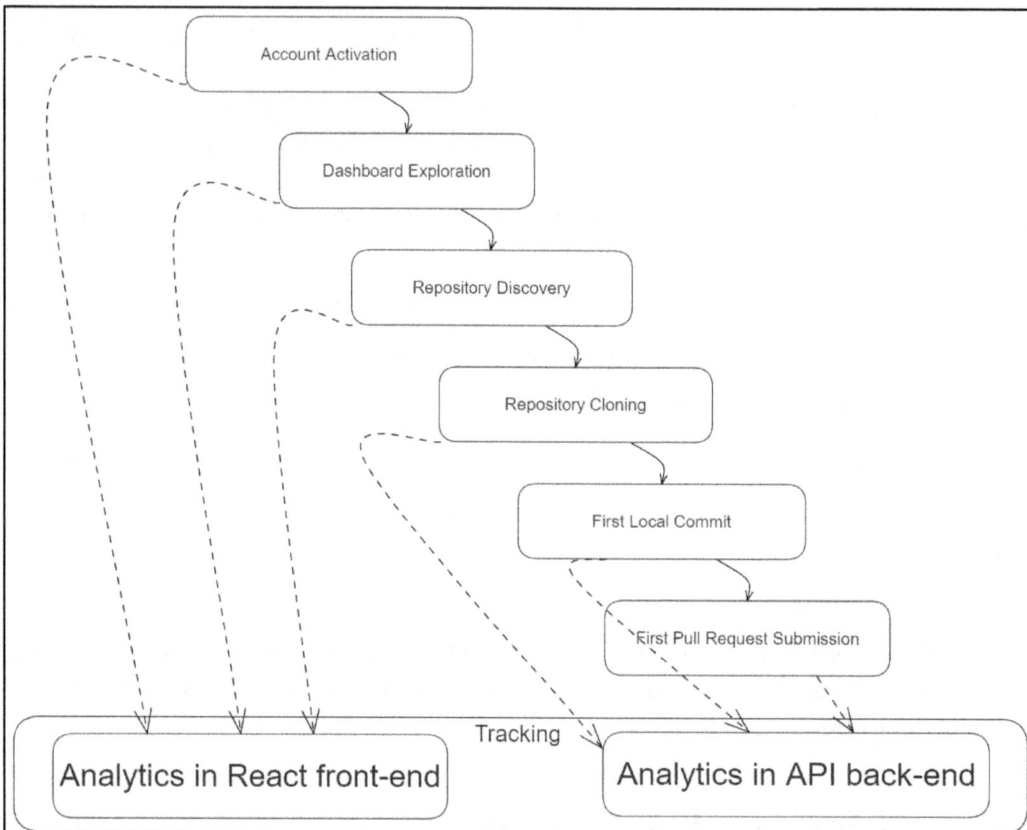

Fig 4.1 Drop-Off Funnel

To track progress and identify exactly where drop-offs happened, the engineering team instrumented analytics events across both ends of the product, front-end React components and back-end API endpoints. This gave them a complete picture of the journey and helped them pinpoint the exact stage where engagement faltered. There are structured properties such as

userId, **sessionId**, **timestamp** and contextual metadata (e.g., **repoId**, **cloneMethod**) allowing granular analysis. At the same time, the automated heatmap tooling captured click, hover, and scroll behavior on the most important UI elements, the "Verify Email," "Clone in IDE," and "Open Pull Request" buttons, providing visual overlays of user engagement.

Conversion Rate Calculations

Using daily event exports into a centralized Redshift warehouse, the analytics team crafted SQL queries to calculate conversion rates and drop-off percentages at each funnel stage over rolling 7- and 30-day windows.

Following is a simplified example:

```
WITH onboarding AS (
  SELECT userId,
    MAX(CASE WHEN event='Email Verified' THEN 1 ELSE 0 END) AS activated,
    MAX(CASE WHEN event='Dashboard Viewed' THEN 1 ELSE 0 END) AS explored,
    MAX(CASE WHEN event='Repo Viewed' THEN 1 ELSE 0 END) AS discovered,
    MAX(CASE WHEN event='Repo Cloned' THEN 1 ELSE 0 END) AS cloned,
    MAX(CASE WHEN event='Local Commit' THEN 1 ELSE 0 END) AS committed,
    MAX(CASE WHEN event='PR Created' THEN 1 ELSE 0 END) AS pr_created
  FROM events
  WHERE timestamp >= CURRENT_DATE - INTERVAL '30 days'
  GROUP BY userId
)
SELECT
  ROUND(100.0 * SUM(explored)/SUM(activated),2) AS activation_to_explore,
  ROUND(100.0 * SUM(discovered)/SUM(explored),2) AS explore_to_discover,
  ROUND(100.0 * SUM(cloned)/SUM(discovered),2) AS discover_to_clone,
  ROUND(100.0 * SUM(committed)/SUM(cloned),2) AS clone_to_commit,
  ROUND(100.0 * SUM(pr_created)/SUM(committed),2) AS commit_to_pr
FROM onboarding;
```

When we first looked at the numbers, it didn't look good. More than 85% of activations were exploration hovers, but only about 50% of those explorations led to discoveries, and less than

30% of discoveries ended up as clones. The commitment and PR rates were pretty low by comparison.

User Interviews and Session Recordings

To go along with the hard metrics, UX researchers did 40 one-on-one sessions with new sign-ups. Screen recordings showed confusion when none of the "Repository" dropdown options matched the expected sample projects. In surveys, users said they got frustrated because they didn't understand the command-line interface and didn't have any clear backup options. A lot of people just closed the browser tab after running into errors in the embedded terminal, and they never went back to CodeHub.

The team figured out six main onboarding problems by putting these signals together:

- The UI labels didn't match the naming conventions in the sample code tutorials.
- Hey, just a heads-up: we're having some trouble cloning because we can't find the setup instructions for the SSH key.
- The most important steps were written in different wiki pages that you couldn't get to without knowing the context.
- Users were faced with their entire workflow all at once, which caused them to feel overwhelmed.
- Since there were no tooltips or chat support, questions remained unanswered.
- The error messages in the command-line interface didn't have links to guides on how to fix the problems.

Designing Targeted Flow Enhancements

With the insights in hand, the team quickly got to work designing fixes that directly tackled the biggest drop-off points in the onboarding flow. First, they introduced a **Dynamic Repository Carousel** which is a sleek horizontal scroll showing featured sample repositories tailored to the user's role and past choices. Then came the **In-Browser Git Setup Wizard**, which is a friendly pop-up that walked the users through SSH key generation, Git configuration, and cloning a repo, and all this without touching the terminal.

To make sure help was always within reach, they added a **Contextual Documentation Panel**, a collapsible sidebar that displayed just-in-time tips right next to the tool the user was working in. The **Step-by-Step Onboarding Tour** guided newcomers through each stage with clear hints and progress markers. Finally, an **Embedded Chat & FAQ Widget** gave users instant access to on-call mentors or quick answers triggered by what they were doing.

Every feature was tested with A/B experiments, carefully tracked with custom analytics. The results were dramatic:

- Explore-to-Discover jumped from 50% to 80%
- Discover-to-Clone rose from 30% to 65%
- Clone-to-Commit climbed from 20% to 50%
- Commit-to-PR doubled from 15% to 40%
- Time-to-First-Clone shrank from **2 days to 4 hours**, and Time-to-First-PR dropped from **5 days to 1 day**.

Once the tests proved their worth, the team rolled out the winning versions to all new sign-ups and even existing users through in-app announcements. They also baked these onboarding improvements into their ongoing experimentation framework, and added a **Time-to-First-PR dashboard** for executives to track.

The impact was huge, as CodeHub's onboarding completion rate skyrocketed from **15% to 60% in just eight weeks**, blowing past the 50% goal. The Git setup wizard alone cut setup pain by 70%, while the carousel and live documentation boosted repo clones by 45%. It was more than just a quick win, it became a repeatable playbook for growth, keeping developer satisfaction and adoption on a strong upward curve.

API & Documentation Playbook

When developers hit a wall in the drop-off funnel, fractured or missing API documentation often lay at the root. To address this, the CodeHub's technical writing and engineering teams partnered to build an API & Documentation Playbook, a centralized, auto-generated system combining live OpenAPI specifications, interactive code snippets and embedded sandboxes. This playbook aimed to streamline the learning curve, reduce support ticket volume and empower developers to self-serve their integration needs.

OpenAPI Specifications

A first critical step was automating the extraction of API schemas directly from CodeHub's microservices. The engineers added Swagger decorators to each service definition, enabling the build pipeline to emit up-to-date OpenAPI 3.0 YAML files.

Following is a sample annotation in the Node.js repository service looked like:

```
/**
 * @openapi
 * /repos/{repoId}:
 *   get:
 *     summary: Retrieve repository metadata
```

```
 *   parameters:
 *     - in: path
 *       name: repoId
 *       required: true
 *       schema:
 *         type: string
 *   responses:
 *     200:
 *       description: Repository object
 */
function getRepo(req, res) {
  // implementation
}
```

The CI job then executed swagger-jsdoc to compile these annotations into a cohesive specification:

```
swagger-jsdoc -d swaggerDef.js -o ./docs/openapi.yaml "src/**/*.js"
```

This above YAML fed into documentation generators (ReDoc, Swagger UI) and a custom React-based portal. As a result, documentation remained in lockstep with the codebase, every merge or feature flag toggle in development triggered an automated regeneration of the API spec.

Live Sandboxes

The static examples often failed to capture dynamic behavior. Now here, to bridge this gap, the team integrated https://codesandbox.io/ embeddable sandboxes directly into the docs pages. Each endpoint section included a "Try It Live" button, launching a pre-configured sandbox environment that preloaded required SDKs, authentication tokens and sample payloads. For instance, the "Create Pull Request" endpoint displayed:

The developers could modify parameters, run requests and inspect real-time responses without leaving the browser. The complementary inline code snippets in JavaScript, Python and cURL provided quick-start examples:

```
curl -X POST https://api.codehub.com/repos/{owner}/{repo}/pulls \
  -H "Authorization: Bearer <token>" \
  -d '{
```

```
  "title": "My new feature",
  "head": "feature-branch",
  "base": "main"
}'
```

We realized that making JSON bodies by hand turned off a lot of users, so the playbook included a curated library of sample payloads organized by use case: repository creation, branch management, webhook setup, and more. There's a collapsible "Copy Payload" button that lets you insert something into documentation or sandboxes with just one click.

Endpoint	Sample Payload Name	Description
POST /repos	**create-repo.json**	Template for new repository creation
POST /webhooks	**setup-webhook.json**	Predefined webhook configuration example
PATCH /repos/{id}/files	**update-file.json**	Sample payload for in-line file updates

Versioning and Release Notes

The APIs evolve, and stale docs erode trust. To keep the playbook current, versioned spec URLs (e.g., **/docs/v1.2.0/openapi.yaml**) corresponded to each semantic release. Release notes, auto-generated from commit messages and PR descriptions tagged with **@release-note**, populated a dedicated changelog section. The developers received email notifications and in-app banners announcing documentation updates, with direct links to diff views.

Within the six weeks of playbook launch, the support metrics showed:

- **50% reduction** in API-related tickets.
- **30% increase** in successful first-time API calls.
- **25% improvement** in Time-to-First-API-Call for new users.

The qualitative feedback in surveys highlighted that 85% of users found the live sandboxes "very helpful," and 70% reported quicker resolution of integration questions.

Framework Components

The **API & Documentation Playbook** is a flexible framework designed to help any developer platform create clear, reliable, and engaging API experiences. It blends automation, interactivity, and continuous improvement to ensure developers can discover, understand, and use your APIs with minimal friction.

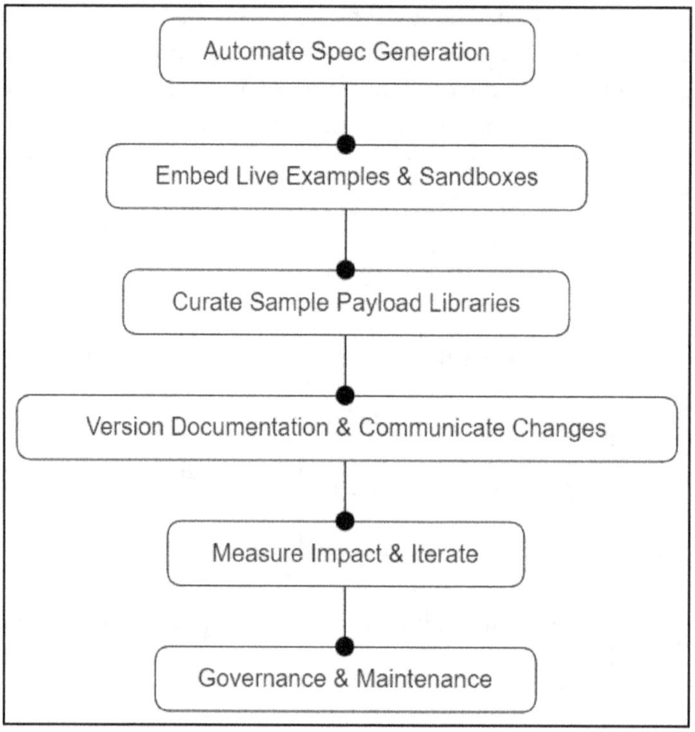

Fig 4.2 Framework Components

Automate Spec Generation

It starts with **automation at the source**. Instead of writing documentation separately, developers annotate their service code with endpoint details, parameters, and response schemas using tools like Swagger, JSDoc, or Springfox. The build pipeline then automatically generates and validates OpenAPI specifications, catching mismatches before they reach production.

Embed Live Examples and Sandboxes

From here, the documentation becomes a living, interactive guide. Every endpoint features live code samples in multiple languages, JavaScript, Python, Go, and cURL, generated directly from the spec. Developers can try these requests instantly in embedded sandboxes like CodeSandbox or StackBlitz, complete with mock servers or real API hooks. Temporary credentials make it safe to experiment without compromising security.

Curate Sample Payload Libraries

Practicality is key, so the playbook includes **curated sample payloads** organized by real-world workflows, such as onboarding, repository management, or webhooks. One-click copy buttons save time, and examples are versioned to match the API release they came from, ensuring they never go stale.

Version Documentation and Communicate Changes

Versioning and change communication are built-in. Documentation follows semantic versioning to match API releases, and changes are communicated through automated changelogs, visual diffs, and developer alerts, whether via in-app banners, newsletters, or RSS feeds, so nobody is caught off guard by breaking changes.

Measure Impact and Iterate

The impact of these practices is constantly measured. Analytics track how often developers view docs, try examples, or copy snippets, and this data feeds into ongoing improvements. Support ticket volume is compared before and after changes to gauge how well the docs reduce developer frustration. Quick feedback tools embedded in the docs, like star ratings and "Was this helpful?" prompts, capture suggestions directly from users.

Governance and Maintenance

Behind the scenes, clear ownership keeps the playbook healthy. Roles are defined for spec stewardship, content curation, and advocacy. Automated linting checks maintain consistent formatting and style, while quarterly audits ensure everything, from sandbox uptime to example relevance, meets a high standard.

When implemented together, these practices transform static documentation into an interactive, living resource that grows with the platform and its users. The result is a documentation playbook that not only accelerates onboarding and reduces support burden but also fosters deep engagement and trust.

Experimentation Framework Setup

When a rapid succession of feature launches led to contradictory feedback, some users praising improvements while others reported regressions, the development team realized that intuition alone could not guide product decisions reliably. A senior developer suggested instituting a formal experimentation framework to replace ad-hoc trials with structured, hypothesis-driven tests. Embracing this feedback, the team crafted a robust plan for multivariate testing spanning onboarding emails, in-app guidance and interactive tutorials.

Formulating Actionable Hypotheses

The tests started with clear, measurable hypotheses linking specific changes to expected user outcomes. Each hypothesis followed this template:

***When** we apply [change X] in [context Y], **then** [metric Z] will move by [target Δ], **because** [insight from user feedback or data].*

Like, when the onboarding email includes a one-click Git Setup Wizard link, then the click-through rate will climb by 25%, because users have indicated difficulty finding setup instructions.

The team documented the reasoning behind each choice and the expected impact, and they did this before any code was written. This made sure that the product, engineering, and analytics teams were all on the same page.

Defining Test Variants and Scope

In each experiment, the team tested between three and five versions of the feature.

The **control group** saw the existing experience with no changes. Other versions introduced different tweaks, some updated the wording or call-to-action text, others changed visual elements like button color, placement, or icons.

A few tests focused on functionality, such as adjusting tooltip timing or adding tutorial prompts. In some cases, multiple changes were combined into a single version to see if they worked better together.

It was a piece of cake to turn each version on or off without having to do a full deployment. Targeting rules made sure that only the right users, like new sign-ups or specific groups, were included in the tests.

Calculating Sample Sizes and Test Durations

The whole point of statistical validity is making sure the sample size and test duration are on point. The analytics team looked at past traffic data to figure out:

- **the Baseline Rate (p_0)** which is the existing conversion percentages for the metric under study.
- **the Minimum Detectable Effect (δ)** which is the smallest relative change worth detecting, typically set between 10% and 20%.
- **the Power ($1-\beta$)** as it is the desired probability (80%) of correctly rejecting a false null hypothesis.
- **and, lastly the Significance (α)** as the acceptable risk (5%) of a false positive.

Using these inputs, an online power calculator determined the required number of users per variant. The team then set test durations to span at least two full business cycles (e.g., two weeks) to account for weekday and weekend behavior patterns.

Data Collection and Analysis

For CodeHub, getting accurate data was critical to making the right decisions.

In email tests, every link included unique tracking parameters so the team could see exactly who opened, clicked, and took follow-up actions, tying each behavior back to the specific email version they saw. Inside the app, the front-end checked feature flags to decide which tooltips or banners to display. Every time a user saw, clicked, or dismissed these, the system logged it along with details like their role and how long they'd been active in that session. Tutorial flows were tracked the same way, every step recorded views, clicks, and completions, all tagged to the version being tested.

All of this data flowed into a single analytics warehouse so results were consistent across tests. Once enough data was collected, the team ran two kinds of analysis. Using **frequentist methods**, they calculated p-values and confidence intervals to see if the difference between variants was statistically significant. Using **Bayesian methods**, they estimated the probability that one version beat another by a meaningful margin.

The decision rules were straightforward:

- **Adopt** a variant if it had at least 95% frequentist confidence or 90% Bayesian probability of outperforming the control.
- **Reject** if it had 95% confidence of underperforming.
- Everything else was **inconclusive** and could be refined or dropped.

This thing let CodeHub innovate faster and with less guesswork, building a library of clear, data-backed insights to shape future features.

Mentorship Rotation Model

Moving on to analytics, when they highlighted that even with improved self-service tooling many new developers still felt isolated during their first week, the CodeHub's leadership sought a way to humanize onboarding at scale. The developer advocacy team had a pretty cool idea: a mentorship rotation model. The plan is to pair each new user with a different senior engineer every two weeks. They think this will help transfer knowledge, build community, and get people working together to solve problems.

Program Goals and Structure

The Mentorship Rotation Model at CodeHub was designed as a structured, people-first initiative to make onboarding faster, more engaging, and more insightful for both new developers and the wider engineering organization.

Its **three primary objectives** set the tone for the program:

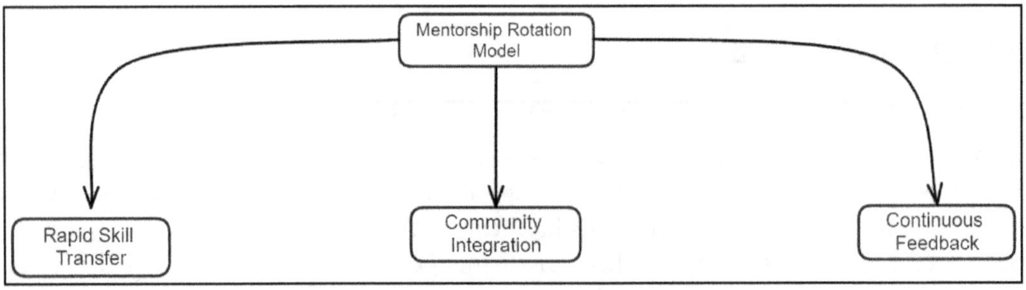

Fig 4.3 Mentorship Rotation Model

- **Rapid Skill Transfer** meant that new developers weren't left to learn the platform on their own. Instead, they participated in guided, hands-on sessions where they could see real workflows in action, try tasks themselves, and receive immediate feedback. These sessions turned complex processes, like setting up CI/CD pipelines or integrating with an API, into approachable, repeatable steps.
- **Community Integration** was equally important. Rather than treating onboarding as an isolated training period, the program intentionally paired new hires with veteran engineers, fostering relationships that extended beyond the rotation itself. These partnerships helped new developers feel like part of the CodeHub culture from day one, and gave them trusted contacts to approach long after the rotation ended.
- **Continuous Feedback** created a feedback loop that benefited the entire organization. Mentors were encouraged to share patterns they noticed, like common setup errors or unclear documentation, so that product and engineering teams could address issues at the source. This not only improved the onboarding process for future hires but also helped refine the platform itself.

Now to achieve these goals, the program followed a **structured rotation cycle**. Each mentee-mentor pairing lasted two weeks, enough time for observation, questions, and gradual task ownership. A pool of ten senior engineers volunteered to serve as mentors, each representing a unique area of expertise, ranging from backend services and front-end development to CI/CD workflows and API design.

New hires were organized into **cohorts of four** to keep the mentorship manageable and collaborative. At the start of each rotation, the mentorship coordinator hosted an **introductory meeting**. Mentors learned about their mentees' backgrounds, technical skills, and personal goals. Mentees, in turn, were briefed on their mentor's specialties and given clarity on availability windows, ensuring expectations were aligned from the start.

Mentorship Pairing Logic

Rather than manually assigning pairings, the team built an automated pairing engine:

1. **Profile Matching:** Each mentor and mentee profile included tags, language preferences, experience domains, time zone availability.
2. **Rotation Algorithm:** A weighted round-robin algorithm assigned mentors to cohort groups, ensuring balanced workloads and exposing mentees to different perspectives over successive rotations.
3. **Conflict Avoidance:** The engine checked calendar availability and throttle limits, preventing overbooking of mentors or burnout.

The pairing logic ran as a scheduled job on Monday mornings, generating assignments for the upcoming two-week window and sending calendar invites automatically.

Curriculum and Activity Framework

Now to provide structure, the program defined a flexible agenda template for each mentor–mentee relationship:

Week	Activities	Deliverables
Week 1, Day 1	Kickoff meeting: introductions, goals alignment	Shared agenda, mentoring charter
Week 1, Day 3	Platform tour: core features, dashboards, common workflows	Annotated feature map
Week 1, Day 5	Hands-on task: small bug fix or feature exploration	Pull request for sandbox project
Week 2, Day 2	Deep dive: codebase navigation, debugging patterns	Code walkthrough notes
Week 2, Day 4	Q&A session: open forum for challenges and design questions	Mentee feedback questionnaire
Week 2, Day 5	Wrap-up: review progress, set next steps and learning goals	Personal learning plan, feedback form

The mentors adjusted the schedule based on mentee needs, but all followed the core framework to maintain consistency.

Feedback Loops and Progress Check-Ins

It was really important to get real-time feedback to make the program better. The team used lightweight survey tools and automated check-ins, such as:

Mid-Rotation Pulse

On Day 7, mentees got a one-question survey. "On a scale of 1 to 5, how supported do you feel?" Any response above 4 triggered an automated thank-you note, and any response below 3 alerted the program coordinator for intervention.

End-of-Rotation Survey

They did a survey with a bunch of questions to see how well the mentors were doing, how clear their guidance was, and what else they needed to learn.

Mentor Logs

The mentors tracked the highlights and challenges that the group faced in a shared doc, helping to spot systemic issues.

All these feedbacks are sent to a main dashboard, where it's separated into groups based on cohorts, mentors, and task types. Every week, we've got these program review meetings with the product and engineering leaders. They take a look at the dashboards and decide on action items, like making improvements to the documentation for topics that keep coming up as confusing.

Pilot Outcomes and Metrics

The eight-week pilot of the Mentorship Rotation Model served as both a trial run and a proof of concept, giving CodeHub concrete data on how structured mentorship could transform the onboarding experience. The program brought together **three cohorts**, a total of 12 mentees, who rotated through a carefully selected pool of **six senior mentors**. These mentors were chosen for their deep expertise across different technical areas and their willingness to invest time in guiding newcomers. Over the course of the pilot, each mentee experienced multiple perspectives, learning not just the "how" of CodeHub's systems but also the "why" behind design and architectural decisions.

From the very beginning, the pilot was designed with **clear, measurable performance indicators**. One of the most striking results was the improvement in **Time-to-First-Pull-Request (TTFPR)**. Before the program, it took new developers an average of five days to submit their first PR. In the pilot, that time dropped to just two days, less than half the baseline, indicating faster skill acquisition and greater confidence in engaging with production code. The **Mentee**

satisfaction scores were equally telling. Across all three cohorts, the average post-program rating came in at **4.7 out of 5**, with feedback highlighting not only the technical gains but also the supportive environment the program fostered.

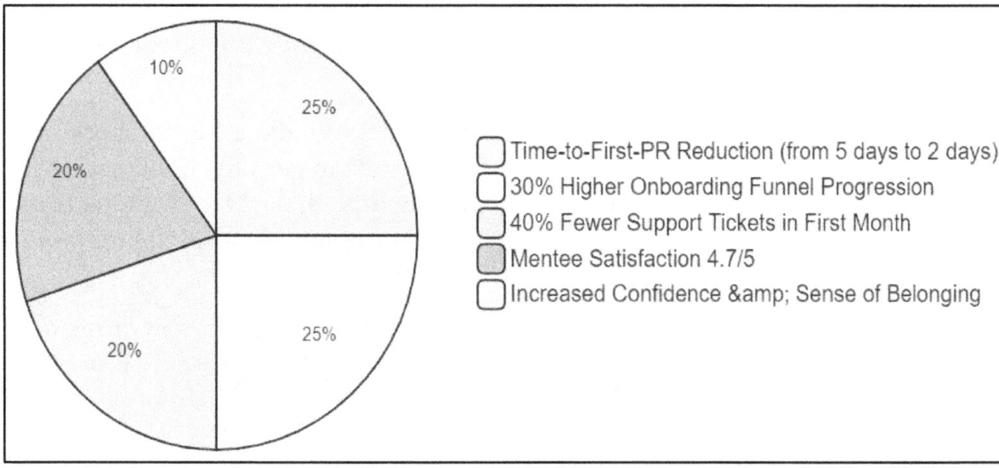

Fig 4.4 Mentorship Pilot Outcome Chart

The mentorship also had a clear ripple effect on the **onboarding funnel**. Mentored participants advanced through the funnel stages, such as repository exploration, cloning, first commit, and first PR, at a **30% higher rate** than peers who went through onboarding without mentorship. The support operations felt the impact too. During their first month, mentored developers filed **40% fewer support tickets** compared to non-mentored sign-ups, suggesting that guided learning significantly reduced confusion and self-service friction.

Beyond the numbers, **qualitative feedback** painted a vivid picture of the program's cultural benefits. Many mentees spoke about the **human connection** the mentorship fostered, how having a go-to person for questions, feedback, and encouragement made them feel more confident in their work and more deeply connected to the CodeHub community. This sense of belonging, combined with accelerated technical onboarding, positioned the program as a powerful tool for both productivity and retention.

Scaling and Continuous Refinement

When the CodeHub team saw how well the pilot worked to improve onboarding, they knew they couldn't stop there. The Mentorship Rotation Model needed to grow, get better, and become a permanent part of how the organization nurtures its talent. They decided to grow the mentor pool. Instead of just having a few senior engineers on board, the program brought in 25 volunteer mentors from all over the company. This expansion included leaders from different teams, like security and QA, making sure mentees could learn from a wider range of expertise and perspectives. The result wasn't just more capacity, it meant a richer, more diverse learning experience for every new developer.

Now, to handle the larger scale without losing the personal touch, the team introduced automated matching powered by machine learning. The system looks at how well past pairings worked out, how much mentees have improved, and feedback scores to suggest the best mentor-mentee pairings. The program also developed a resource library to help mentors get up to speed quickly and provide consistent, high-quality guidance. This library had mentor handbooks, slide decks you could just use, and sample schedules for two-week rotations.

We made measurement the foundation of the scaled model. We did a health check every three months to keep an eye on important stuff like how long it took to get a first pull request (TTFPR), how many support tickets were filed by users who were mentored, the Net Promoter Score (NPS) for the mentorship experience, and how many mentors we kept around. These reports kept leadership in the loop and gave them a heads-up if something needed tweaking.

With such Mentorship Rotation Model firmly established, the CodeHub now turns to defining and tracking Time-to-First-Pull-Request metrics in depth, the final frontier in their comprehensive onboarding transformation.

Time-to-First-Pull-Request Metric

Since the Mentorship Rotation Model was such a hit, the CodeHub leaders figured out that measuring how fast developers went from making an account to contributing something useful would be a good way to see how well onboarding is working. This metric, Time-to-First-Pull-Request (TTFPR), shows the time between when a user signs up and when their first pull request is merged. They've been using CodeHub to measure, analyze, and visualize TTFPR across different groups and projects. This has given them a powerful tool to identify bottlenecks, validate improvements, and set performance goals for ongoing excellence.

Definition and Its Significance

TTFPR serves as a proxy for several intertwined outcomes:

- The user's ability to navigate developer workflows and use CodeHub's features effectively.
- The clarity of setup instructions, documentation and in-app guidance experienced during early interactions.
- The efficacy of peer support, whether through the Mentorship Rotation Model or embedded chat.
- The absence of technical errors or permission barriers that can stall first contributions.

The team realized that a single number wouldn't cover everything, so they decided on two definitions that worked well together:

1. TTFPR (Registration-Based): The time from when the account was created to when the

first pull request was merged.

2. TTFPR (First Interaction-Based): From the time you first log in to the dashboard to the time the first merged pull request is sent, including any delays from logging in or email verifications.

With this, the analytics team could distinguish between friction in account activation versus friction in productive usage.

Data Collection and Calculating TTFPR

To get the right measurements, we need to link events together from the authentication, UI analytics, and version control systems. The engineering team did the following:

The engineering team started by tagging critical milestones in the platform. The first was the **Registration Event**, recorded as **user_registered**. This was triggered the moment a new developer successfully signed up and confirmed their email via the authentication service. Next came the **Dashboard View Event**, tagged as **dashboard_viewed**, which fired when the user first landed on the main UI, their starting point for exploring repositories and tools. Finally, the **Pull Request Merge Event** was captured directly from the Git backend, including details like the user ID, PR ID, repository ID, and a timestamp marking the moment their work officially became part of the codebase.

All events are streamed into the analytics warehouse via Kafka, and they're enriched with user traits (role, cohort, referral source) and session context (device, region). This real-time data pipeline allowed the team to **refresh key metrics every hour**. That meant fast feedback loops, issues could be spotted almost immediately, and progress could be tracked without waiting days or weeks for results.

Then, the analytics team wrote some solid queries to calculate daily, weekly, and cohort-filtered TTFPR statistics. Following is a simplified example:

```
WITH first_events AS (
  SELECT
    ur.userId,
    MIN(CASE WHEN event='user_registered' THEN timestamp END) AS registration_time,
    MIN(CASE WHEN event='dashboard_viewed' THEN timestamp END) AS
first_view_time
  FROM user_events ur
  WHERE ur.event IN ('user_registered','dashboard_viewed')
  GROUP BY ur.userId
),
```

```
first_pr AS (
  SELECT
    p.userId,
    MIN(p.merged_at) AS first_pr_time
  FROM prs p
  GROUP BY p.userId
)
SELECT
  fe.userId,
  EXTRACT(epoch FROM (fp.first_pr_time - fe.registration_time)) / 3600 AS
hours_to_first_pr_reg,
  EXTRACT(epoch FROM (fp.first_pr_time - fe.first_view_time)) / 3600 AS
hours_to_first_pr_view
FROM first_events fe
JOIN first_pr fp ON fe.userId = fp.userId
WHERE fe.registration_time >= CURRENT_DATE - INTERVAL '30 days';
```

This query yielded hour-level precision on both definitions, and then aggregating it across users produced distribution curves, percentiles and averages for reporting.

Visualizing TTFPR

To really understand **Time-to-First-Pull-Request (TTFPR)**, the analytics team built a set of clear, visual reports, such as:

- A **TTFPR Histogram** that shows how many hours it took different users to make their first PR, with markers for the median, 75th percentile, and 90th percentile.

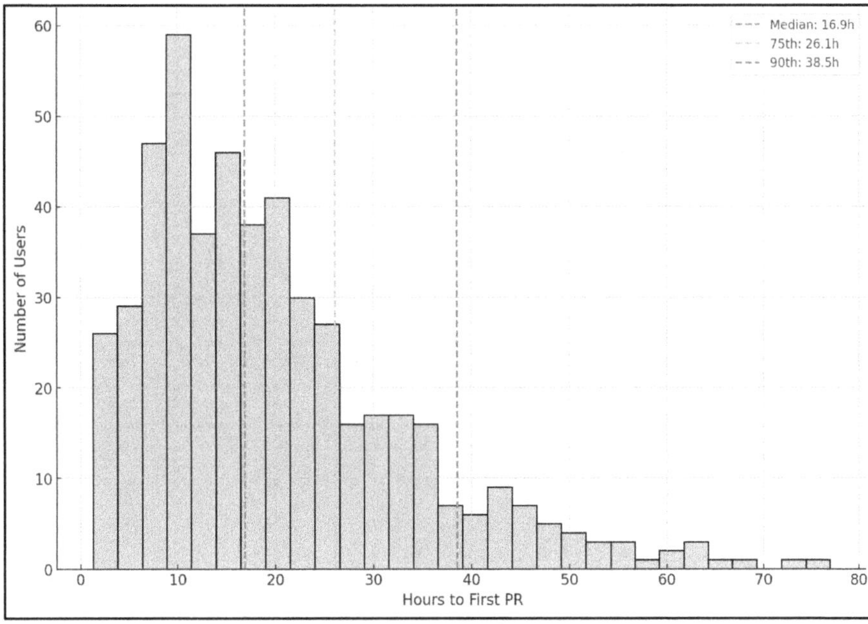

Fig 4.5 TTFPR Histogram

- A **Cohort Curve** tracking the percentage of each group (e.g., before vs. after mentorship) managed to merge a PR within certain timeframes.

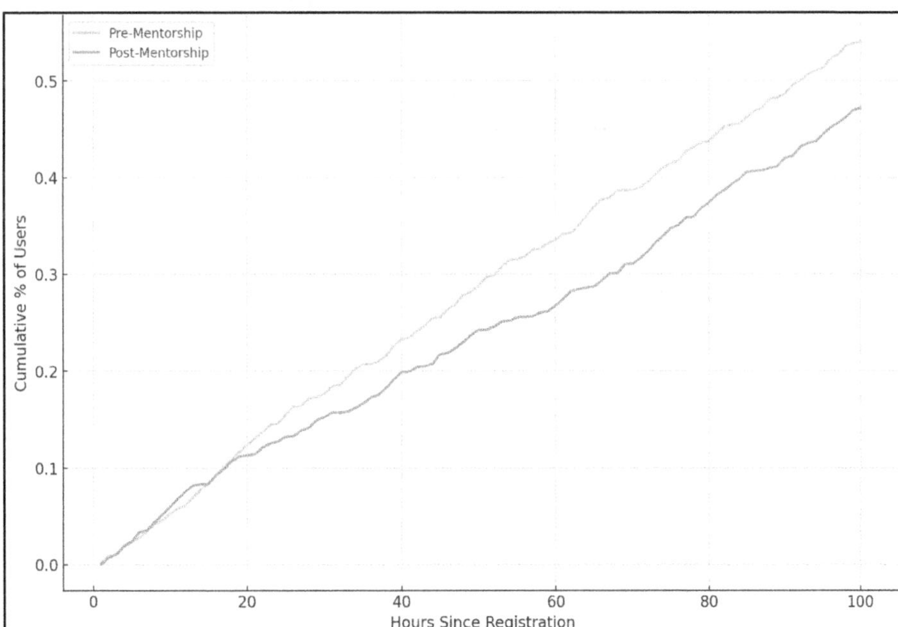

Fig 4.6 Cumulative Merging Users – Cohort Analysis

- There is a **Trend Line** that displays the rolling 7-day average TTFPR over time, with notes showing when major initiatives launched, so the team can see what actually made an impact.

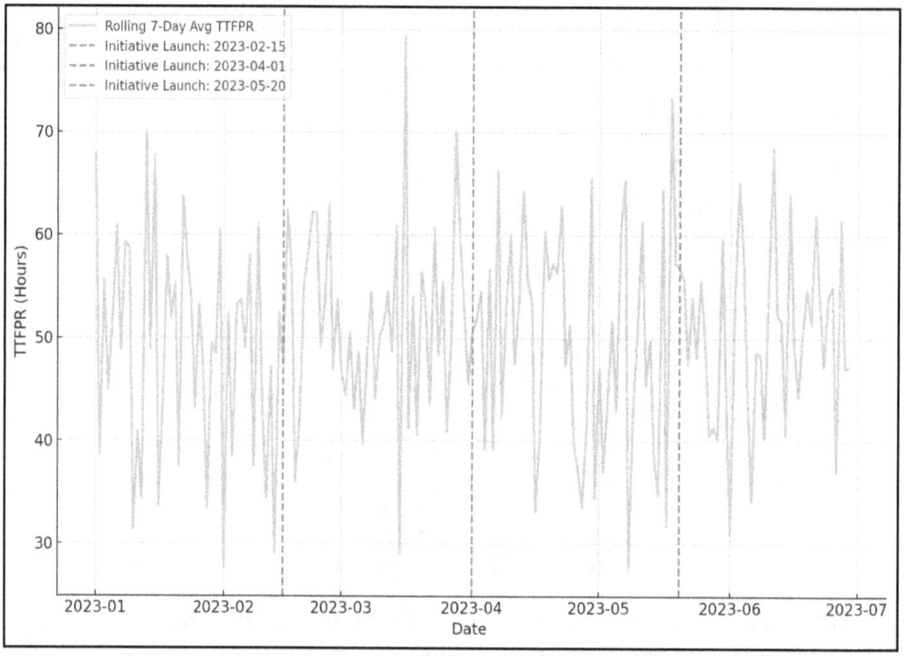

Fig 4.7 Seven-Day Average TTFPR Trends

- And, there is the last **Funnel Overlay** that puts the TTFPR stats right on top of the onboarding funnel, so it's clear how delays in any stage affect overall time to first PR.

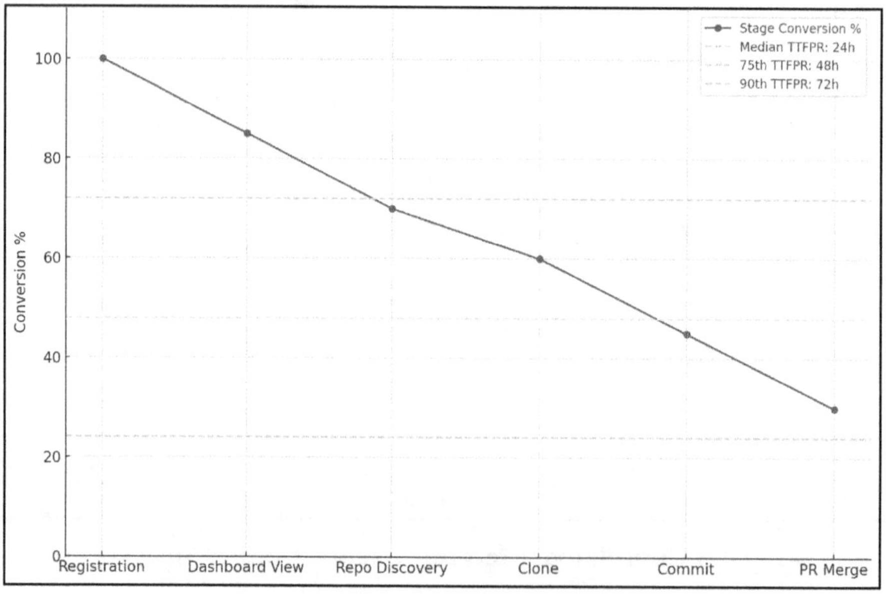

Fig 4.8 Funnel Conversion Overlay

All of these appear together in a **central Looker dashboard**, updated in real time and accessible to product managers, engineers, and executives, making it easy to connect the dots between changes, user behavior, and outcomes.

Targets, SLAs, and Improvements

With baseline TTFPR measured at a median of 72 hours (registration-based) and 48 hours (view-based), the leadership defined quarterly targets:

Metric	Baseline	Target (Q1)	Target (Q2)
Median TTFPR (Reg-Based)	72 hrs	≤36 hrs (-50%)	≤24 hrs (-67%)
90th Percentile TTFPR (View-Based)	96 hrs	≤48 hrs (-50%)	≤36 hrs (-63%)

These targets drove prioritization of onboarding improvements and mentorship expansions. Automated alerts monitored deviations, notifying the growth and product teams when trends faltered.

Beyond the overall metrics, breaking things down further revealed some hidden insights:

- We found that external contractor referrals had a median TTFPR of 120 hours, compared to 60 hours for internal employees. This led us to create custom onboarding flows for contractors.
- The mentees in the first rotation cohort had a median TTFPR of 24 hours, which is three times faster than non-mentored users.
- We've also highlighted higher TTFPR on certain mobile devices, which has led to UI performance optimizations.
- We saw an initial spike in TTFPR during the first week of the major UI overhaul, which is helping us plan the rollouts.

These deep dives led to specific action plans, like making tutorials for contractors and improving the mobile web IDE. SO, the team combined these TTFPR analyses with feedback loops, and with good efforts, the team uncovered specific friction points, such as:

- Users took an average of 8 hours to verify email, accounting for 10% of TTFPR delay.
- The new developers often stalled during Docker setup, adding 12 hours.
- And, almost 7% of first PRs failed due to missing write permissions.

By quantifying the time impact of each obstacle, product teams could prioritize fixes based on hours saved per user.

It's all about defining, measuring, and acting on the Time-to-First-Pull-Request metric. CodeHub closed the loop on its comprehensive onboarding initiative by doing this, turning raw user activity into actionable insights. This method made sure that every improvement, from automated tutorials to human-led mentorship, led to a clear increase in developer proficiency. With clear visibility into time-to-first-PR trends, the team can now pinpoint emerging bottlenecks, validate new features in real time, and set ambitious yet attainable goals for future cohorts. In the end, this metric became the platform's guiding light, leading to incremental improvements and ensuring that developers were happy and that the platform was adopted for the long term.

Case-Study Freebies

To accelerate your experimentation efforts, here are two ready-to-use spreadsheet canvas templates. Copy into Excel, Google Sheets or any PM/analytics tool:

Experiment Tracker

Test Name	Hypothesis	Variant Details	Success Metric	Duration	Owner
Streamlined PR Editor	Simplifying the pull request editor will reduce cognitive load and increase PR submissions by ≥20%.	Control, Minimalist UI, Enhanced Linting & Templates	Median TTFPR (hours)	4 weeks	[PM Name]
In-Editor Mentorship Prompts	Real-time chat prompts during PR creation will lower TTFPR by ≥20% through immediate support availability.	Control, Static Tooltip, Chat Widget Variant	Median TTFPR (hours); Chat Engagement Rate	4 weeks	[Dev Advocate]

Onboarding Email Wizard	Including a one-click Git Setup Wizard link in onboarding emails will boost wizard CTR by ≥25%.	Control, Copy Update, Wizard Link	Email CTR; Time to First Clone (hours)	3 weeks	[Growth Lead]
Contextual Help Sidebar	Embedding docs sidebars in the clone interface will raise clone-to-commit conversion by ≥30%.	Control, Sidebar A, Sidebar B	Clone-to-Commit Conversion (%)	3 weeks	[UX Lead]

Post-Experiment Review

Experiment ID	Variant A vs B	Sample Size	Result Summary	Statistical Significance	Next Steps
EX-001	Control vs Enhanced UI	12,000	Variant B reduced TTFPR by 25%; error rate unchanged.	p<0.01	Roll out globally; monitor support.
EX-002	Tooltip vs Chat Widget	10,500	Chat widget variant showed 30% faster PR completion.	p<0.05	Expand chat widget to other flows.
EX-003	Email A vs Email B	8,000	Email B increased click-through by 28%; no uplift in PRs.	p=0.07 (inconclusive)	Iterate on email copy; retest.
EX-004	Tutorial A vs Tutorial C	9,200	Tutorial C improved commit rate by 35% and	p<0.005	Adopt Tutorial C for all

			reduced errors.		cohorts.

Bring together your **PMs, analysts, engineers, and designers** for a quick 30-minute workshop.

- Open the **Experiment Tracker** template on a shared screen.
- Walk through each field (Hypothesis, Variants, Metrics, etc.) together.
- Make sure *everyone* understands the test goal before anyone starts building.

Instead of writing vague "we think it will be better" statements:

- Ask the group: **"What exactly will improve, by how much, and why?"**
- Fill in the Hypothesis column together, making it measurable (e.g., *Reduce TTFPR by ≥20%*).
- Agree on what counts as a win before you code a single line.

Once the test idea is locked in:

- Work with engineering to **set up feature flags** for each variant.
- Decide the rollout schedule and "kill switch" conditions so you can revert quickly if needed.
- Link the spreadsheet to your analytics dashboard or embed it directly.
- Turn on **alerts** so if a metric drop (e.g., click-through rate tanks), the team knows right away.
- Keep the live dashboard visible in your "war room" or Slack channel.

Halfway through the test:

- Hold a quick 10-minute check-in to share early numbers.
- If something's broken, fix it now, don't wait until the end.
- Adjust traffic splits if one variant is obviously underperforming.

When the test ends:

- Use the **Post-Experiment Review** template to compare results.
- Show lift curves or side-by-side charts so it's easy to see the winner.
- Capture feedback right there in the spreadsheet, what worked, what didn't, and what to try next.
- Add follow-up ideas straight into the tracker so they don't get lost.

- Assign owners for the next tests.
- Update your roadmap to show when the next experiment cycle starts.

If you follow this process, which is interactive and team-driven, you'll get the most alignment, learn the fastest, and maintain transparency across all stages of experimentation.

Measuring Pin Engagement for a Visual Network

Background

PinPoint's visual discovery platform empowers users to curate, organize and share images and videos, known as "pins", across personalized boards. As the platform scaled into millions of pieces of content, pin engagement became a key indicator of both user satisfaction and business health. While account growth and board creations rose steadily, leadership noticed that daily active pinners and average session durations plateaued. High-level metrics such as total pins saved or monthly active users offered limited visibility into the subtleties of user behavior, specifically, how deeply users engaged with pin actions like saving, sharing and discovery.

To address this gap, the PinPoint launched a focused initiative to develop a comprehensive analytics and experimentation framework centered on pin engagement. The objectives were to:

1. Articulate the business intent behind "save" and "share" workflows.
2. Connect feature enhancements to measurable engagement uplifts.

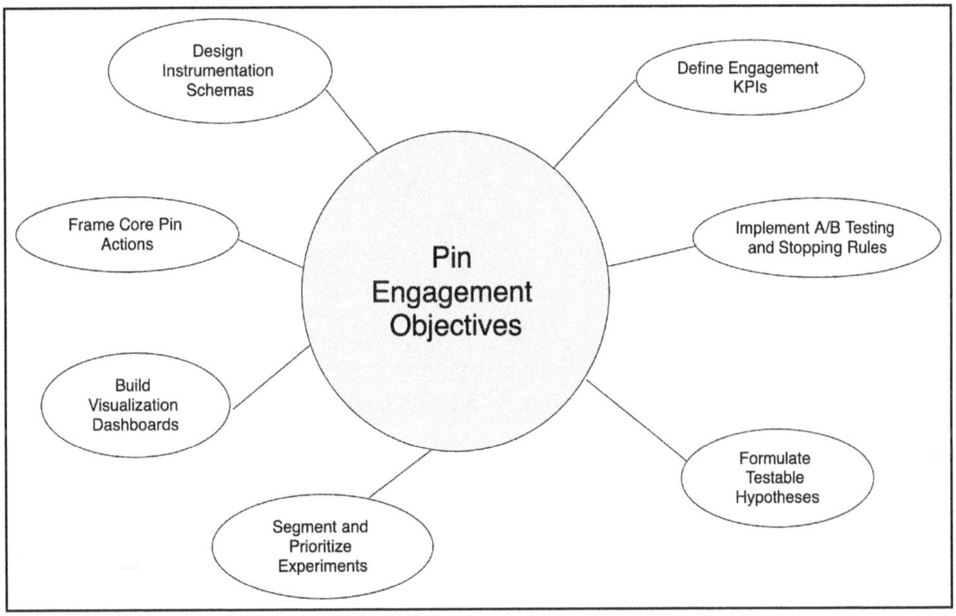

Fig 5.1 PinPoint's Pin Purpose

3. Align tests with high-impact user cohorts and resource constraints.
4. Capture granular events with contextual metadata.
5. Establish leading and lagging indicators for retention and growth.
6. Ensure statistical rigor and clear decision gates.
7. Provide real-time insights to cross-functional teams.

We now dig into the first phase, **Feature Framing and Hypotheses**, detailing how PinPoint structured its business intent and developed hypotheses to guide targeted experimentation on the platform's core engagement mechanisms.

Feature Framing and Hypotheses

The PinPoint's value proposition is rooted in two primary user actions:

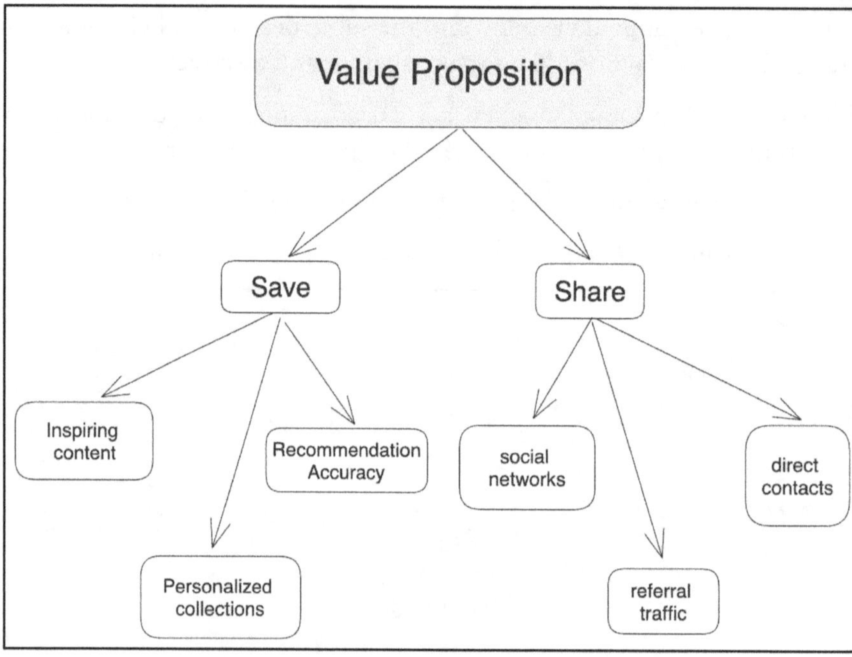

Fig 5.2 PinPoint's Value Proposition

- **Save** to allow users to bookmark inspiring content for future reference, fueling personalized collections and improving recommendation accuracy.
- **And, share** to empowers users to distribute content to social networks or direct contacts, driving referral traffic and expanding the platform's reach.

Articulating Testable Hypotheses

For each feature, the team drafted hypotheses in a structured format:

- **When** the one-click save button is available on pin hover, **then** daily saves per active user will increase by 15%, **because** users no longer need to hunt for the save control.
- **When** the inline share menu appears upon pin hover, **then** overall share counts per day will grow by 20%, **because** share options are surfaced at the moment of inspiration.

The secondary hypotheses captured downstream effects:

- **If** daily saves increase by ≥15%, **then** average session duration will extend by ≥10%, **because** users spend more time exploring saved collections.
- **If** share counts rise by ≥20%, **then** new user registrations from shared links will grow by ≥5%, **because** shares drive referral traffic.

These clear, measurable statements ensured alignment across product, engineering and analytics teams.

Defining Variants and User Segments

Now here, each experiment included:

- **Variant A** which has a new UI element enabled without copy changes.
- And, there is another **Variant B** which is a UI element with enhanced microcopy.

And the user segments for allocation:

- **Power Pinners** are those users with ≥10 saves in the past week.
- **Casual Browsers** having session frequency 1–2 per week.
- **New Referrals** are the sign-ups arriving via shared links.

This segmentation enabled tailored analysis of feature impact across distinct user behaviors.

Mapping Metrics to Hypotheses

Each hypothesis paired with primary and secondary metrics:

Hypothesis Context	Primary Metric	Secondary Metrics
One-Click Save	Daily Saves per Active User	Session Duration; Multi-Session Return Rate
Inline Share Menu	Daily Share Counts	Referral Sign-Ups; Board Followers Increase
Enhanced Microcopy	Button Click-Through Rate	Save/Share Conversion Rate; Time to First Action

These metrics formed the backbone of subsequent instrumentation schema design.

Prioritizing Experiments with a Scoring Model

To allocate resources effectively, the PinPoint evaluated each hypothesis on three criteria:

1. **Impact Potential (50%)** which is a projected lift in core KPIs based on benchmark data.
2. **Implementation Effort (30%)** is the estimated dev and QA hours (Small, Medium, Large).
3. **Risk Assessment (20%)** is the potential for negative user response or technical regression.

With framing and prioritization complete, the team moved into instrumentation schema design, defining event structures, payload schemas and data pipelines to capture each pin interaction precisely. This foundational work set the stage for robust A/B tests, KPI tracking and real-time dashboards, ensuring PinPoint could measure feature impact with clarity and confidence.

Instrumentation Schema Design

The PinPoint team knew that precise measurement was key to their experiments, as discussed earlier. They decided to use one set of instruments for every save, share, and discovery event, along with the relevant metadata and tracking options. This made sure that the frontend and backend implementations worked well together and that each testable hypothesis could be validated with confidence.

The schema design is laid out below in full, with info on event naming conventions, payload structures, metadata fields, versioning strategies, validation rules, and collaboration checkpoints.

Event Naming Conventions

Consistent event names reduce ambiguity and simplify downstream analytics. The PinPoint adopted a hierarchical, verb-driven pattern:

<Category>.<Action>.<Context>

In this, the Category is the high-level feature area (e.g., Pin, Board, User, Share). The Action is the user or system activity (e.g., Clicked, Created, Viewed, Errored). And, the Context is the optional qualifier for additional detail (e.g., Button, Modal, Carousel).

Following are some of the examples:

- **Pin.Clicked.Button**, user clicked the save button on a pin.
- **Share.Created.Popover**, user initiated a share action via the inline share popover.
- **Board.Viewed.Page**, user viewed a board's main page.

Event Payload Structure

Each event payload followed a standardized JSON schema:


```json
{
  "event": "Pin.Clicked.Button",
  "timestamp": "2025-08-02T10:15:30Z",
  "userId": "abc123",
  "sessionId": "sess789",
  "properties": {
    "pinId": "pin456",
    "boardId": "board321",
    "pageLocation": "home_feed",
    "referrerPinId": "pin123",
    "device": {
      "type": "mobile",
      "os": "iOS 14.7",
      "appVersion": "3.2.1"
    }
  },
  "context": {
    "language": "en-US",
    "experimentVariant": "oneClickSave_A",
    "trackingVersion": "v2"
  }
}
```


In the above code,

- **event** is the qualified event name.
- **userId, sessionId** are the unique identifiers from the auth and session services.
- **properties** are the core event-specific metadata, with an explicit schema per event type.

- **context** is the system-level metadata, including A/B variant tags, SDK version and locale.

Metadata Fields and Schemas

The PinPoint defined a canonical set of metadata fields common across all events, and event-specific property schemas:

Field	Type	Description
language	string	User's locale (e.g., **en-US**).
experimentVariant	string	Active A/B test variant identifier.
trackingVersion	string	Schema version (e.g., **v1**, **v2**).
referrer	string	Page or feature that referred to this action.

Each of the schema was captured in a JSON Schema document stored in the analytics repo, enabling code generation and automated validation.

Below is a simplified flow illustrating how a **Pin.Clicked.Button** event travels through the system:

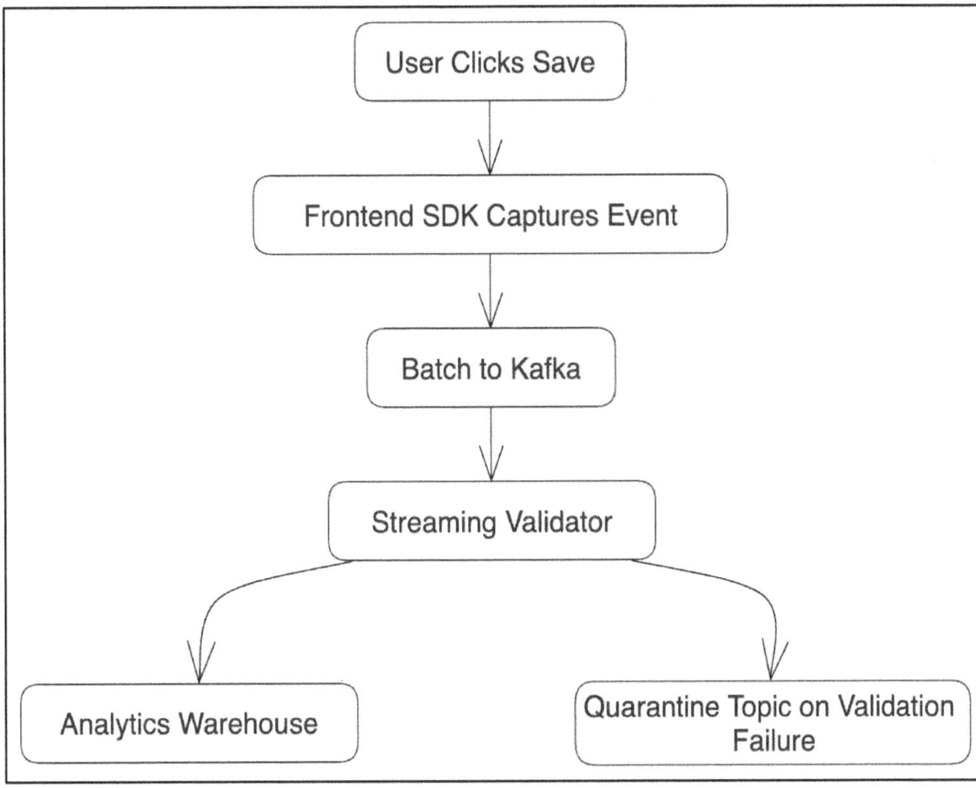

Fig 5.3 Pin Journey

Real-Time ETL and Dashboards

The validated events streamed into a real-time analytics cluster like a Redshift or Snowflake. The ETL jobs transformed raw events into fact tables:

- **`fct_pin_actions`**, fact table recording every pin action with foreign keys to user, board and session dimensions.
- **`dim_event`**, dimension table enumerating event types, schema versions and property definitions.

The Business intelligence dashboards utilized these tables to compute conversion funnels, time-series trends and cohort analyses, driving continuous insights into pin behavior and experiment outcomes. With event data flowing seamlessly into reports, the PinPoint is poised to progress into the next phase of its engagement framework, refining dashboards further and exploring deeper analytics to support subsequent experimentation and KPI tracking steps.

Core vs. Vanity Metrics

In the months following the instrumentation rollout, the PinPoint's analytics team accumulated a wealth of data on pin interactions. However, the sheer volume of available metrics threatened to overwhelm product decision-makers. Early dashboards displayed hundreds of charts, total pins saved, daily share counts, average board sizes, session lengths, heatmap click densities, video play rates and more. Leadership recognized that without rigorous filtering and classification, the organization risked chasing noise rather than actionable insights.

Core Engagement Metrics

Core metrics (also known as "actionable metrics") directly tie to business objectives and user behaviors that drive retention, growth or monetization. The PinPoint identified a set of foundational KPIs around pin functionality:

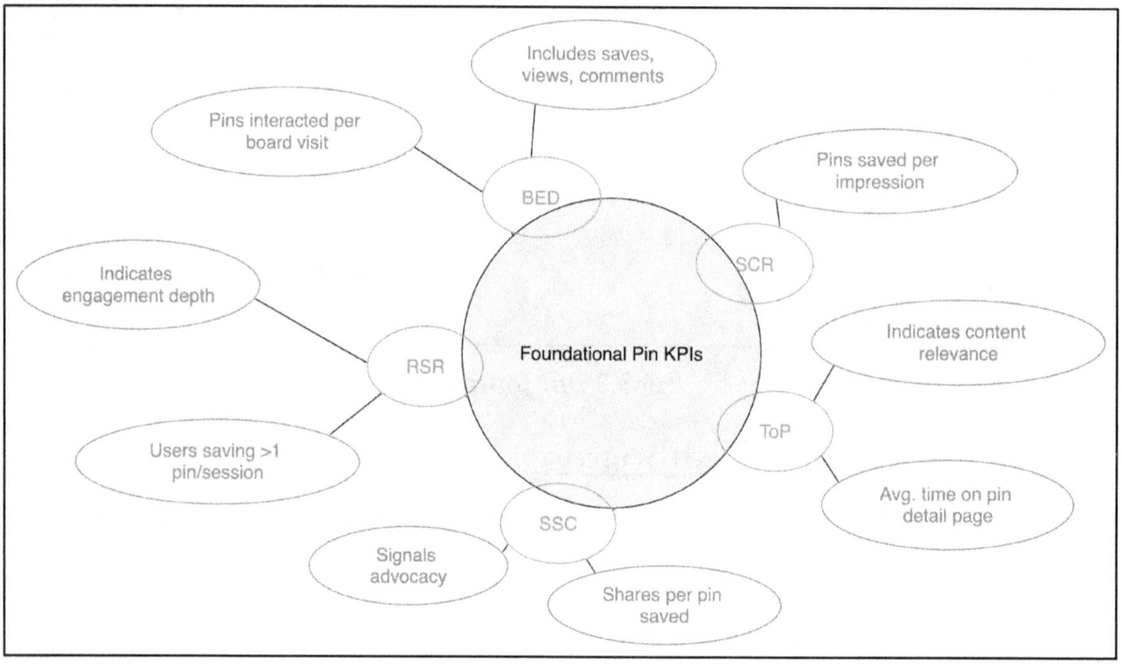

Fig 5.4 Core Pin KPIs

These core metrics were selected because they:

- Directly influence recommendation algorithms, referral growth and ad targeting.
- Each can be decomposed by device, cohort, content category and experiment variant.
- Are sensitive to UI tweaks, feature launches and onboarding improvements.

Recognizing Vanity Metrics

The vanity metrics, by contrast, reflect surface-level volume counts without necessarily indicating healthy user engagement or long-term value. There are common vanity metrics that

PinPoint's teams flagged are:

- **Total Pins Saved** which is a cumulative number of pins saved platform-wide.
- **Monthly Active Users (MAU)** which is nothing but the count of unique logins per month.
- **App Downloads** are the number of installs irrespective of user activity post-install.
- **Total Board Creations** is the volume of new boards without regard to subsequent engagement.

While these numbers can be encouraging, often highlighted in press releases, they offer limited guidance on whether users discover meaningful content, return to the platform or generate revenue. For example, an uptick in MAU driven by one-off browsing sessions may inflate active-user counts but mask stagnating depth of engagement or poor retention.

Contrasting Core and Vanity Metrics

To illustrate the distinction, the analytics team prepared the following comparison using dummy data for a typical week:

Metric	Value	Interpretation (Core)	Interpretation (Vanity)
Total Pins Saved	1,200,000	N/A	Shows raw volume but not quality of engagement
Save-to-Click Ratio (SCR)	12%	Indicates effectiveness of pin design and placement	Not directly inferred from total saves
Monthly Active Users (MAU)	500,000	N/A	May include dormant or low-engagement users
Repeat Save Rate (RSR)	28%	Reflects depth of user engagement on boards	Not captured by board creation volumes
Board Creations	80,000	N/A	Does not indicate board usage after creation

A superficial reading of total pins saved and MAU could suggest that engagement was healthy, while the core metrics SCR and RSR revealed opportunities to boost genuine user involvement.

Extracting Meaningful Patterns

By plotting core versus vanity metrics together on time-series charts, the PinPoint uncovered revealing patterns:

Scenario A: Feature Release Spike

Following is the scenario A data:

week	total_pins_saved	MAU	SCR
7	116.43	1034.3286187499998	0.11928143903999998
8	115.27	1029.1569756562499	0.11904287616191998
9	114.12	1024.0111907779685	0.11880479040959614
10	112.97	1018.8911348240787	0.11856718082877694

After deploying the one-click save button (Week 4), Total Pins Saved jumped by 20%, and MAU increased by 5%. However, SCR improved from 10% to 12%, a modest 2-point lift. RSR and BED showed only 3% and 2% gains respectively, indicating that while more pins were being saved, deeper, repeat engagement did not scale equivalently. This signaled the need for complementary features (e.g., board recommendations) to convert superficial saves into sustained exploration.

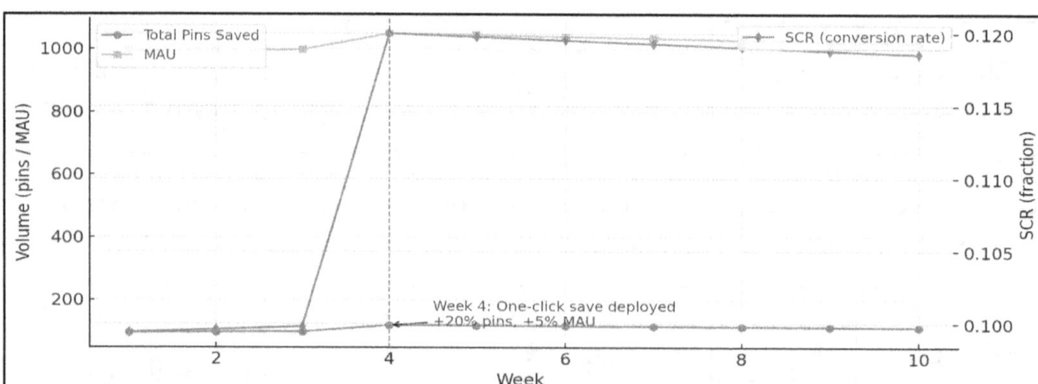

Fig 5.5 Feature Release Spikes (Week 4)

Scenario B: Marketing Campaign

Following is the scenario B data:

week	MAU	total_board_creations	SCR
1	1000.0	50.0	0.12
2	1000.0	50.1	0.11964
3	1002.0	50.2	0.11928
4	1002.0	50.3	0.11892
5	1004.0	50.4	0.11856
6	1004.0	50.5	0.1182

A major influencer partnership in Week 7 led to a 30% surge in MAU and a 15% increase in Total Board Creations. Yet SCR dipped from 12% to 9%, and Share-to-Save Conversion fell by 5%. Though vanity numbers soared, core engagement weakened, prompting a reassessment of campaign targeting.

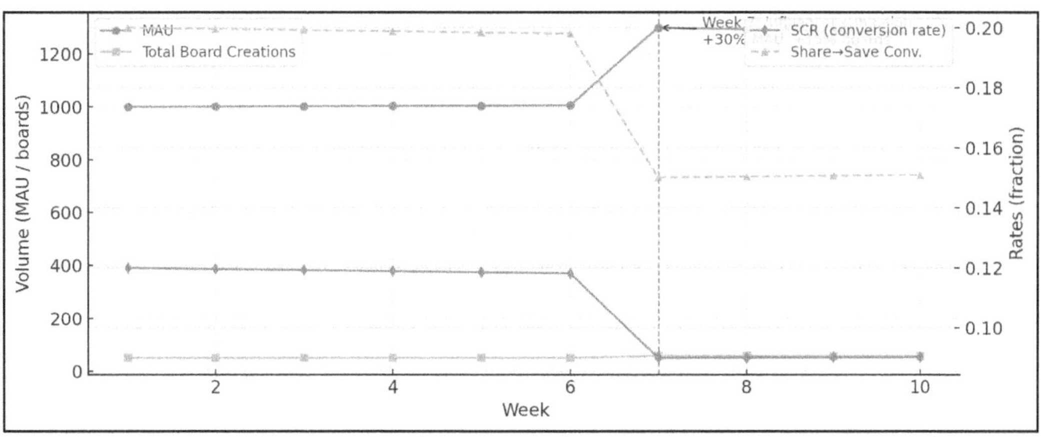

Fig 5.6 Marketing Campaign (Week 7)

The PinPoint formalized a metric evaluation framework with four dimensions:

1. An **actionability** check asks whether the team can influence the metric through product changes.
2. A **correlation** to business outcomes check verifies if metric movement lines up with retention, referral growth, or revenue.
3. A **sensitivity** to change assessment determines if the metric responds quickly enough to reveal effects from experiments or feature launches.
4. An **ease of measurement** test confirms the metric can be computed reliably with existing instrumentation and with minimal lag.

The metrics scoring high across all four dimensions were deemed core, while those lacking in one or more were relegated to supporting or vanity status. To guide stakeholders, the analytics team created infographics that juxtaposed core and vanity metrics.

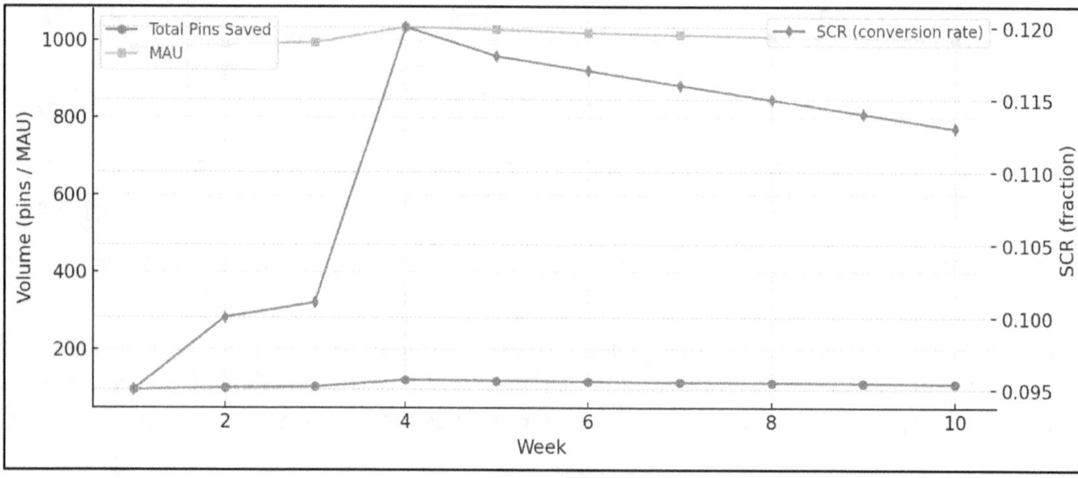

Fig 5.7 Total Pins Saved and MAU with SCR

The above chart is a dual-axis time-series overlaying the Total Pins Saved and MAU with SCR on the right axis so divergence during events is visible.

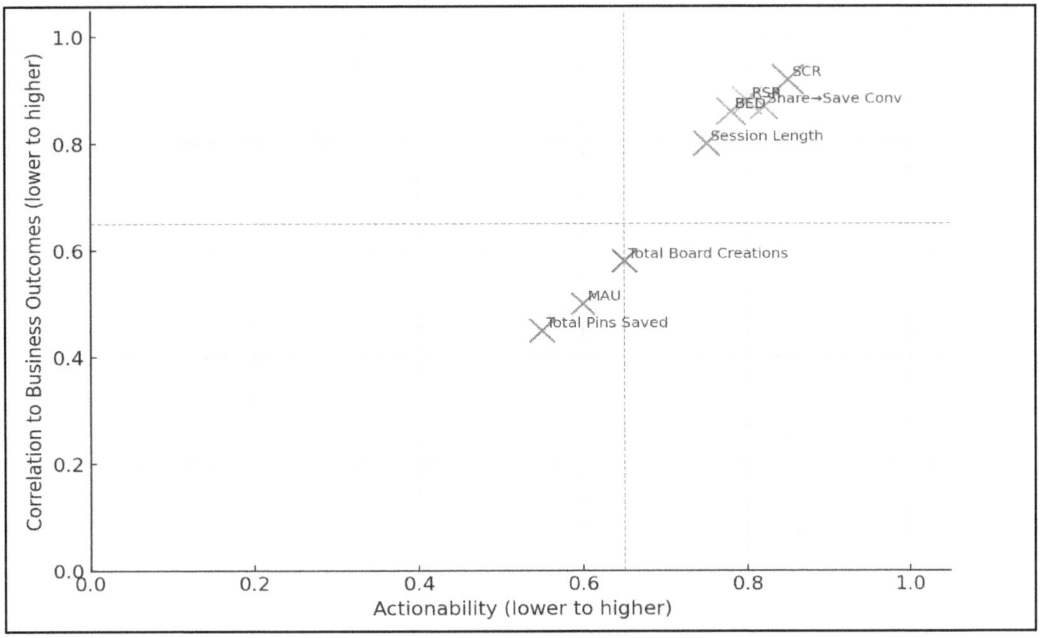

Fig 5.8 Candidate Metrics Scatter Chart

This one is the scatter of candidate metrics by Actionability (x) and Business Correlation (y), with marker size representing Sensitivity and quadrant lines highlighting the top-right core region.

Metrics-Driven Decisions

With core engagement metrics calibrated, the PinPoint's leadership translated data signals into strategic roadmap shifts. Rather than chasing raw volumes, they focused on metrics that held the greatest business leverage:

Board Recommendation Engine Overhaul

Analysis of Repeat Save Rate (RSR) and Board Engagement Depth (BED) following the one-click save rollout revealed that users saved content but seldom explored beyond their initial boards. To deepen engagement, product managers prioritized a reimagined recommendation engine. Guided by segment-level RSR and SCR (Save-to-Click Ratio), engineering teams built an algorithm that surfaced related boards and trending pins. Early A/B tests with a 10% user cohort showed a 15% lift in multi-board visits and a 20% increase in BED, validating the data-driven pivot.

Targeted Referral Incentive Strategy

While the inline share feature boosted Share-to-Save Conversion (SSC) superficially, deeper analysis showed that referrals did not consistently convert into active pinners. Core metrics uncovered a 5% drop in referral activation rate despite a 25% jump in share volume. In response, growth teams paused blanket incentive campaigns and introduced personalized referral codes tied to board themes. Subsequent core metric monitoring registered a 12% increase in referral conversion, confirming that quality-oriented referral mechanics outperform volume-driven tactics.

Phased Video Pin Adoption

Video pins held promise for richer storytelling, but early Time-on-Pin (ToP) and SCR data from beta cohorts indicated mixed results: Power Pinners engaged deeply, but casual browsers exhibited lower save rates. Instead of a wholesale rollout, the PinPoint deployed video pins first to high-SCR segments, using cohort-specific dashboards to monitor performance. Successful indicators, ToP above 30 seconds and SCR above 10%, triggered a gradual expansion to broader user groups, ensuring measured growth without compromising overall engagement metrics.

By anchoring decisions on these core metrics, the PinPoint avoided the allure of vanity numbers and steered product development toward features that demonstrably enhanced user engagement and platform health.

A/B Test and Stopping Rules

After setting up core engagement metrics and running some feature experiments, the PinPoint team came up with a plan for A/B testing, complete with statistical stopping rules to make the most of their resources.

Designing Biweekly Test Rhythm

To foster rapid learning while maintaining analytical rigor, the PinPoint adopted a two-week cycle for A/B experiments. Each cycle encompassed planning, execution, analysis and decision phases:

Phase	Duration	Activities
Planning	2 days	Define hypothesis, variants, metrics and sample-size calculations.
Instrumentation & QA	3 days	Implement feature flags, event tracking and validation checks.

Test Execution	7 days	Run experiment, monitor data quality, ensure consistent traffic split.
Interim Checkpoint	Day 4	Evaluate early signals; decide on continuation or early stop.
Final Analysis	2 days	Conduct full statistical analysis, generate report.
Decision & Rollout	2 days	Approve complete rollout, schedule next experiments.

This above biweekly cadence balanced speed with statistical needs, ensuring that no more than two concurrent experiments ran per team to avoid overlapping impacts and user fatigue.

Calculating Minimum Sample Sizes

The statistical validity hinged on detecting meaningful effects with confidence. For each test, the team calculated the required sample size per variant using the following parameters:

- **Baseline Conversion Rate (p_0):** Historical metric value (e.g., 12% SCR).
- **Desired Lift (Δ):** The minimum detectable effect (e.g., +10% relative uplift).
- **Statistical Power (1-β):** Set to 80% to minimize type-II errors.
- **Significance Level (α):** Fixed at 0.05 (95% confidence).

Using an online calculator or in-house Python script, they derived some sample counts. For example, with $p_0=0.12$ and $\Delta=0.10\times p_0=0.012$:

```
from statsmodels.stats.power import NormalIndPower

analysis = NormalIndPower()

required_n = analysis.solve_power(effect_size=0.012/0.12, power=0.8, alpha=0.05, ratio=1)

print(int(required_n))  # ~10,200 per variant
```

This result meant each arm needed ~10,200 users to achieve sufficient power. Given PinPoint's weekly active user base of 200,000, the seven-day execution window provided ample traffic to satisfy sample-size requirements for both control and variant groups.

Defining Confidence Thresholds and Metrics

For decision-making, the team agreed on these statistical rules:

- **Win** condition wherein the p value less than 0.05 and observed lift at or above the target Δ, so the variant is accepted.
- **Lose** condition wherein the p value less than 0.05 but observed lift below the target, so the variant is rejected.
- **Inconclusive** if the p value 0.05 or higher, so evidence is weak; either iterate the variant for another test or retire it.

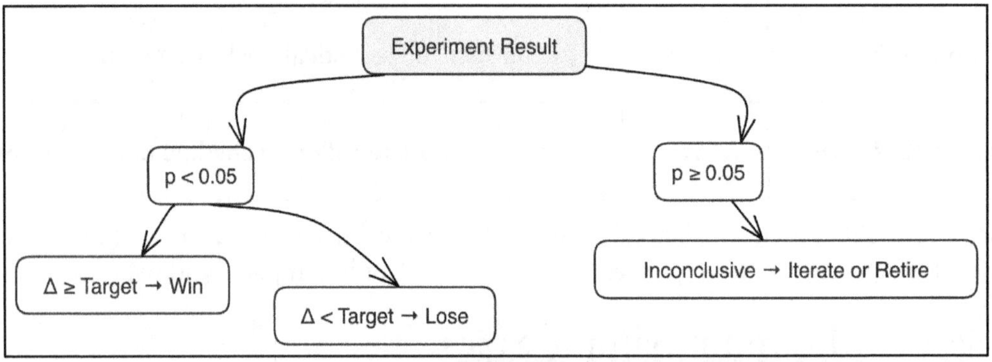

Fig 5.9 Experiment Result Thresholds

The metrics monitored included primary conversion rates and secondary engagement signals. For each experiment, the analytics dashboard displayed real-time z-scores and p-values alongside point estimates and confidence intervals.

Following are the quick visuals that might help to decide faster:

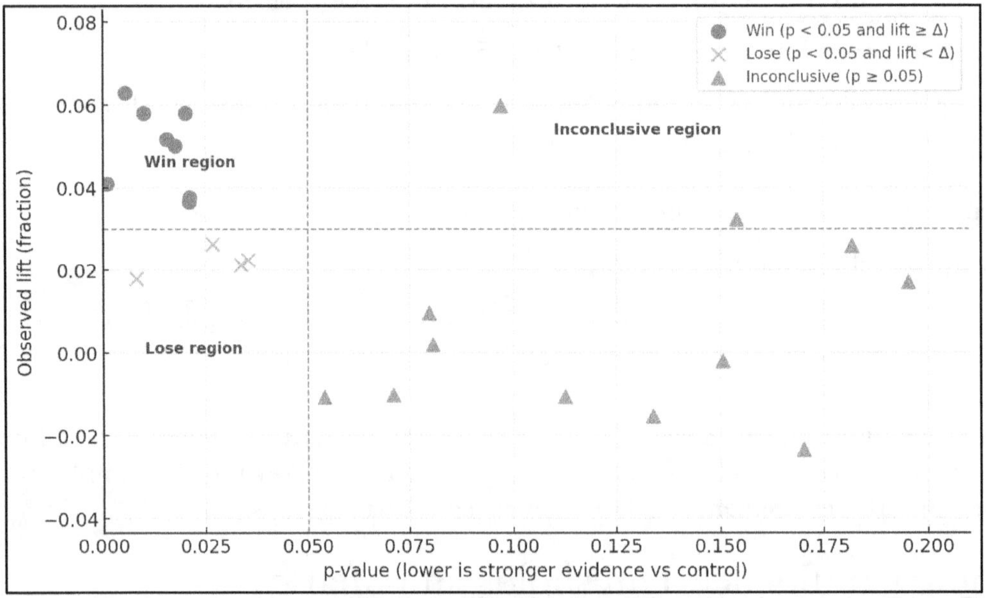

Fig 5.10 Decision Chart

Early Stopping Rules

Now here, midway through each two-week experiment, the team paused to assess emerging signals rather than waiting for the full sample. Four days into the test, when roughly half of the planned participants had experienced both control and variant experiences, analysts ran a comparative z-test to see if the new feature was already making a decisive difference. If the statistical evidence was compelling enough, an interim p-value below 0.005 indicating the variant outperformed control by at least the minimum detectable effect, the experiment was halted early and the winning variant promoted immediately. Conversely, if the data clearly favored the control condition under the same threshold, the test was abandoned to conserve development and user resources. When results fell into an inconclusive range, the team continued collecting data until the scheduled conclusion of the two-week cycle. This sequential style, inspired by group sequential designs, ensured swift wins without sacrificing scientific rigor.

Multiple Concurrent Tests

However, as the volume of simultaneous experiments increased, the PinPoint took care to maintain isolation between tests. Each experiment was assigned distinct user cohorts or unique randomization keys so that any individual's interactions belonged to one test only. Analytics pipelines were partitioned accordingly, and a centralized dashboard tracked the status and sample coverage of every active test, helping stakeholders avoid cross-test interference and ensuring clear attribution of results.

Periodically, the team reviewed early-stop accuracy by comparing interim decisions against full-sample outcomes. Any discrepancies prompted recalibration of p-value thresholds or exploration of alternative statistical techniques such as Bayesian sequential testing. Sample-size formulas were updated to reflect shifting baseline rates, and retrospectives surfaced opportunities to streamline instrumentation and analysis workflows. Through these continuous improvements, the PinPoint maintained a balance between experiment velocity and analytical precision, reinforcing a culture of rapid yet reliable innovation.

Visualization Dashboard Templates

Fresh from their early-stop successes and metric refinements, the PinPoint team turned to crafting dashboards that would bring their data to life. Rather than static reports, they envisioned interactive canvases in Google Looker that would allow product owners and engineers to explore pin engagement in real time. Three signature layouts emerged, each designed to tell a specific part of the story:

Save/Share Funnel Analysis

A vertical funnel chart tracks a cohort of 10,000 users through the steps of pin engagement:

step	count	pct_of_prev
Impressions	10000	100.0%
Clicks	3200	32.0%
Saves	1200	37.5%
Shares	480	40.0%
Referral Sign-Ups	96	20.0%

Following is the Pin engagement funnel having cohort of 10,000 users:

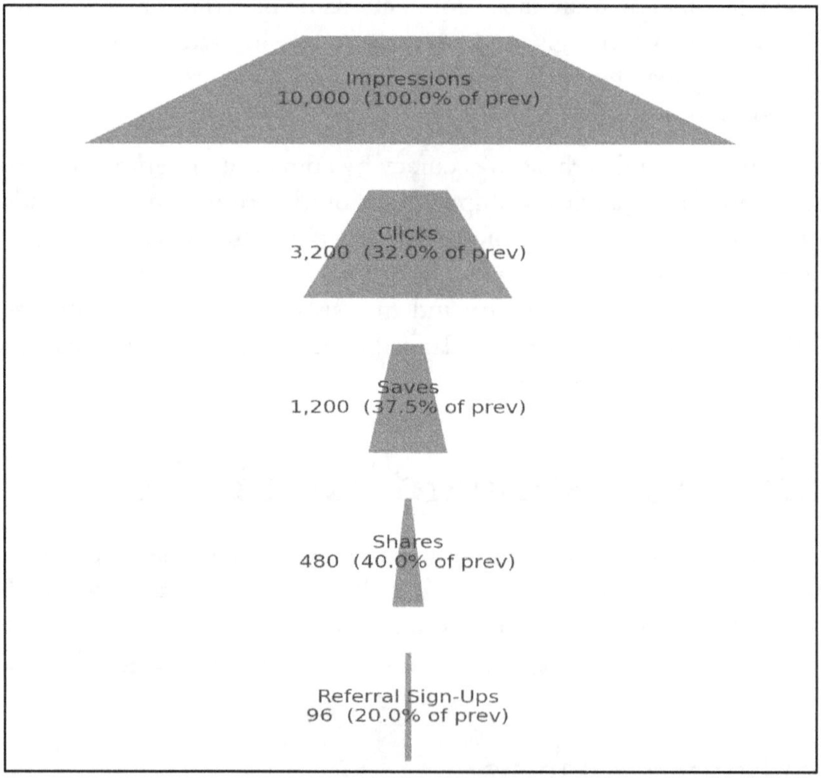

Fig 5.11 Funnel Analysis

In Looker, the team used a single funnel visualization component, mapping each stage count and annotating drop-off percentages between levels. Color gradients, from deep blue at the top to light cyan at the bottom, made the shrinking conversion evident at a glance.

Cohort Retention & Engagement Matrix

A grid shows how four signup cohorts (Weeks 1–4) behave over their first 30 days. Each cell combines retention rate and core engagement:

Cohort/Day	Day 1 Retention	Day 7 Retention	Day 30 Retention	SCR Day 7	SSC Day 7
Week 1	82%	50%	25%	14.0%	5.0%
Week 2	80%	48%	23%	13.5%	4.8%
Week 3	85%	53%	28%	15.2%	5.3%
Week 4	88%	55%	30%	16.0%	5.7%

Using Looker's table visualization, the team applied conditional formatting: cells with retention above 50% or SCR above 15% turned green, quickly spotlighting the highest-performing cohorts as shown below:

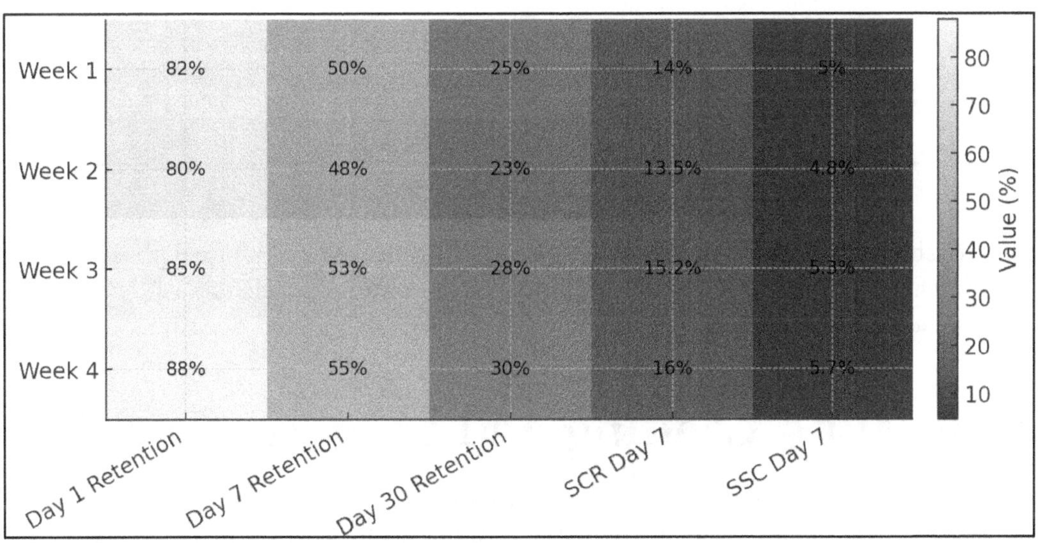

Fig 5.12 SCR/SSC Cohort Grid

Time-Series with Experiment Milestones

To correlate feature releases with metric shifts, the team plotted rolling 7-day averages for SCR and SSC over eight weeks. For example, let us take the following sample data:

Week	1	2	3	4	5	6	7	8
SCR (%)	12	12.5	13	12.8	13.5	14	13.9	14.2
SSC (%)	4	4.2	4.8	5	5.3	5.5	5.2	5.7

In Looker, the line charts for each metric shared the same time axis. Vertical markers flagged experiment start dates (one-click save launched in Week 3, inline share in Week 6). Annotations displayed early-stop decisions, giving context to sudden upticks or plateaus. Interactive tooltips revealed exact values on hover.

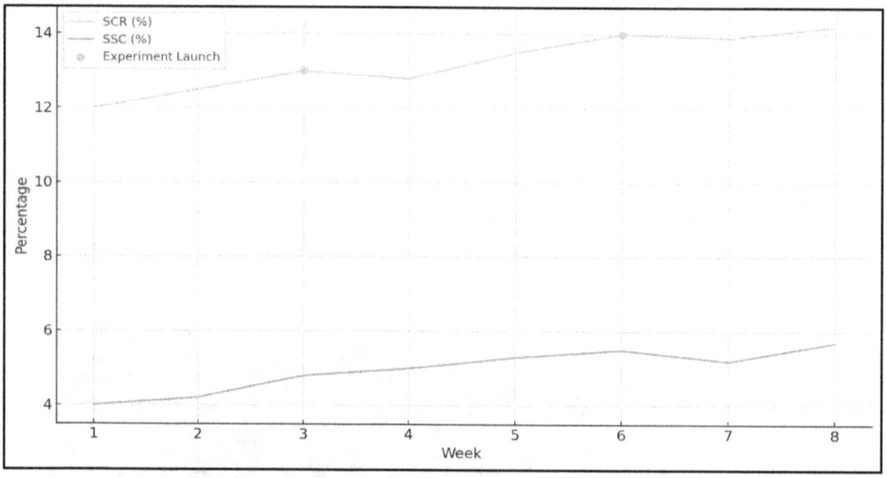

Fig 5.13 Time-Series Rolling Average

With these dashboards in place, the PinPoint was ready to move into the final phases: automating reporting pipelines, sharing insights across teams, and iterating on dashboard designs based on user feedback, ensuring that data continued to drive every pin-focused decision.

Recalibrating Leading and Lagging Signals

In the weeks following the launch of their core dashboards and experimentation cadence, the PinPoint's analytics council recognized that true product health lay not in static, retrospective figures but in forward-looking signals, leading indicators that presaged sustained engagement. To bridge this insight, the team convened a series of cross-functional workshops and during one such workshop, the product manager presented a stark contrast: over the past month, Total Pins Saved had climbed a steady 15 percent, yet retention curves beyond day seven barely budged. Conversely, cohorts exhibiting modest initial growth in Save-to-Click Ratio (SCR) in the first 48 hours showed markedly higher 30-day return rates. This observation sparked a reframing: while raw save volumes (a classic lagging metric) painted a rosy picture, small uplifts in early SCR, observed within the first two app sessions, served as a reliable leading indicator for broader stickiness.

Armed with this revelation, the team mapped the correlations between various metrics over rolling four-week windows. They discovered that:

- A 1.5-point increase in SCR within 48 hours correlated with a 7 percent lift in 30-day retention ($R^2 = 0.78$).
- Users who performed more than one save within their first session generated 20 percent more referral shares over the first week ($R^2 = 0.65$).
- A 10 percent increase in BED during week one translated into a 12 percent increase in average session length by day 30 ($R^2 = 0.71$).

These strong correlations underscored the importance of elevating leading signals, like SCR-growth and ERSR, into primary dashboard positions, while relegating pure volume counts to secondary contexts.

Validating Assumptions through Cohort Analysis

To ensure these correlations held across user segments, the team ran a series of dummy-cohort analyses. They partitioned users by signup source (organic vs. referral) and device type (mobile vs. web) and recalculated correlation coefficients:

Cohort	SCR Growth vs. Retention (R^2)	ERSR vs. Referral Activity (R^2)
Organic-Mobile	0.80	0.60
Organic-Web	0.75	0.62
Referral-Mobile	0.82	0.68
Referral-Web	0.70	0.55

Across all cohorts, the leading indicators maintained strong predictive power, validating their generalizability.

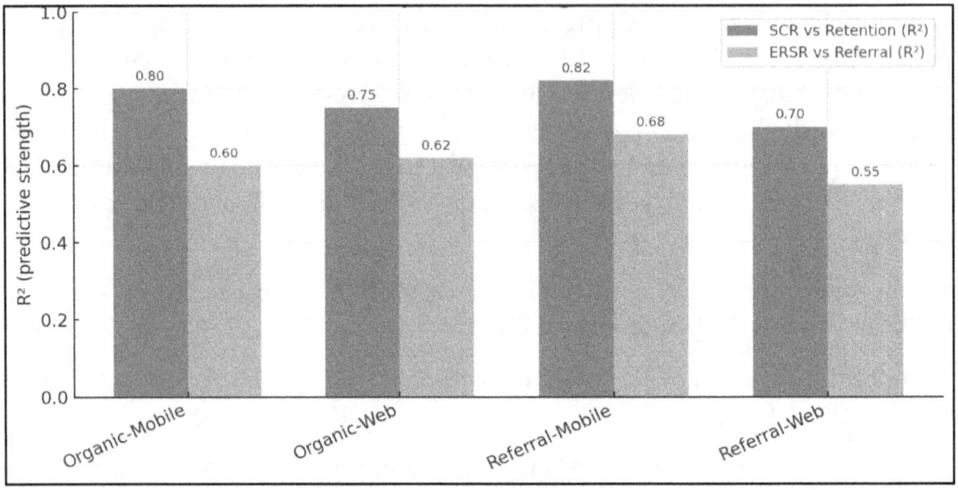

Fig 5.14 Cohort Analysis

There are slight cohort variations guided targeted optimizations, for example, enhancing mobile onboarding flows for web referrals where correlation dipped slightly.

Data Pipeline Adjustments

To support the new visualizations, the engineering team extended ETL pipelines to ingest and compute early-session metrics:

```
-- Calculate 48-hour SCR growth per cohort
WITH sessions AS (
  SELECT user_id, MIN(event_time) AS first_session
  FROM user_events
  WHERE event = 'Dashboard.Viewed'
  GROUP BY user_id
),
first_48h AS (
  SELECT ue.user_id,
       SUM(CASE WHEN ue.event = 'Pin.Clicked.Button' THEN 1 ELSE 0 END) AS clicks,
       SUM(CASE WHEN ue.event = 'Pin.Saved' THEN 1 ELSE 0 END) AS saves
  FROM user_events ue
  JOIN sessions s ON ue.user_id = s.user_id
```

```
  WHERE ue.event_time BETWEEN s.first_session AND s.first_session + INTERVAL '48 hours'
  GROUP BY ue.user_id
)
SELECT
  ROUND(100.0 * SUM(saves) / NULLIF(SUM(clicks),0),2) AS scr_48h
FROM first_48h;
```

Dummy results over four weeks produced a scr_48h array: [11.2, 12.5, 13.0, 14.1], which then fed into Looker tiles displaying both value and trend arrows.

Now, to operationalize leading signals, the team configured Looker to send alert notifications when SCR-48h dipped below 12 percent for two consecutive days. These alerts triggered automatic Slack messages to the growth and product squads, prompting swift assessment, whether that meant launching an A/B test on button placement or iterating microcopy.

Beyond dashboards, the shift to leading indicators fostered a cultural transformation. Engineering standups incorporated a "metric of the week," often a leading signal, to keep the focus on forward-looking performance. Workshops educated stakeholders on interpreting correlation heatmaps and understanding the difference between correlation and causation. This collective fluency in reading predictive metrics galvanized the entire organization around true product health.

Case-Study Freebies

Below is a ready-to-use metric reference template that PinPoint product managers employed. Copy into your analytics or PM tool to align your own metrics:

Metric Name	Definition	Data Source	Calculation Formula
Save-to-Click Ratio (SCR)	Percentage of pin impressions resulting in a save action	**fct_pin_actions**	**(SUM(saves) / SUM(impressions)) * 100**
Share-to-Save Conversion (SSC)	Percentage of saved pins that are shared	**fct_pin_actions**	**(SUM(shares) / SUM(saves)) * 100**

	externally		
Repeat Save Rate (RSR)	Proportion of sessions where a user saves more than one pin	**fct_pin_actions, dim_session**	**COUNT(DISTINCT session_id WHERE saves > 1) / COUNT(DISTINCT session_id) * 100**
Board Engagement Depth (BED)	Average number of distinct pin interactions (views, saves, comments) per board visit	**fct_board_actions**	**SUM(interactions) / COUNT(DISTINCT board_visit_id)**
Time-on-Pin (ToP)	Average dwell time (in seconds) on pin detail pages	**fct_pin_timing**	**AVG(detail_exit_time - detail_enter_time)**
Early SCR Growth	Change in SCR during the first 48 hours post-signup	**user_events**	**SCR_48h - SCR_baseline** (calculated via rolling window SQL)
30-Day Retention	Percentage of users active at least once within 30 days of signup	**dim_user, user_events**	**COUNT(DISTINCT user_id WHERE event_time <= signup+30d AND event=active) / COUNT(DISTINCT user_id) * 100**

At first, point each metric to the specific event or fact table that holds its raw signals so the source of truth is explicit and auditable, and capture the exact column names, timestamp field, and any join keys alongside a short note explaining why that table is authoritative. After the source is fixed, implement the calculation in the place you will maintain it long term, whether that is a SQL view, a stored procedure, or a calculated field inside your BI tool, and test the expression on a small date window to validate edge cases such as late-arriving events, duplicate rows, or null values; keep a short test script or query that reproduces the calculation so others can confirm results.

Track every change to a metric definition with a lightweight version tag and a one-line changelog entry that records who changed what and why, and keep copies of prior SQL or formula text so rollback is straightforward if downstream reports are affected. When wiring metrics into dashboards use consistent names, clear units, fixed aggregation windows, and a canonical date dimension so charts across reports align; prefer explicit aggregation in the metric definition rather than ad hoc aggregation in every chart to avoid accidental mismatches.

Finally, treat this as a living set of definitions and schedule a quarterly review to validate instrumentation, retire metrics that no longer map to business needs, add new signals surfaced by products or experiments, and reassign ownership when people move roles so the metric catalogue stays trustworthy and actionable.

This structured canvas ensures clarity around what you measure, how it's computed and where it originates, empowering your teams to drive decisions based on reliable, actionable metrics.

ESTIMATING SEARCH VOLUME FOR A LEADING ENGINE

Background

SearchStat is no stranger to scale. Every second, millions of people around the world tap into its search engine, whether it's a teenager asking a voice assistant for homework help, a commuter scanning the news via video snippets, or a designer snapping a visual search for a product idea. The ways people search have multiplied, and so has the complexity of understanding what's really happening on the platform at any given moment. The leadership team knew that, in a business where milliseconds matter, simply counting searches wasn't enough. They needed a living, accurate pulse on **total search volume in real time**, and not just globally, but broken down by region. Even more, they wanted to know **how often each user searches**, a metric that could reveal whether the platform was becoming a daily habit or an occasional stop. These numbers wouldn't just sit in a dashboard. They would shape how server clusters were scaled, how network routes were optimized, how advertising revenue was forecasted, and what executives told the market about SearchStat's growth story.

But there was a hitch. The company already collected raw query logs from every data center, but turning that firehose of information into clear, reliable insights was another matter. The naive approach, aggregating all server logs, would be computationally massive and far too slow for the split-second decisions SearchStat needed to make. The existing pipeline introduced **hours of latency**, meaning yesterday's trends often became today's bottlenecks before anyone knew about them. Worse yet, the seemingly simple "searches per user per day" metric was misleading. Heavy "power users" could flood the average with outsized activity, making it look like everyone was searching far more often than they actually were. Casual users, the silent majority, were getting lost in the numbers, creating a distorted view of engagement. In short, the SearchStat had **a measurement problem in the middle of an era where measurement meant survival**.

Estimation Strategy

They needed a faster, smarter way to estimate total search volumes and per-user query rates, something accurate enough for executives to trust, but quick enough to guide real-time decisions. Scanning every log entry wasn't realistic; it was slow, resource-heavy, and not designed for live insights.

So, the analytics and data engineering teams decided to tackle it step by step:

Start with smart sampling

Instead of combing through every single log, the team would take a statistical sample of queries to estimate daily and hourly volumes.

Set clear assumptions

They defined what they believed about user activity, like how peak hours differed from quiet times, and built 95% confidence ranges around their estimates.

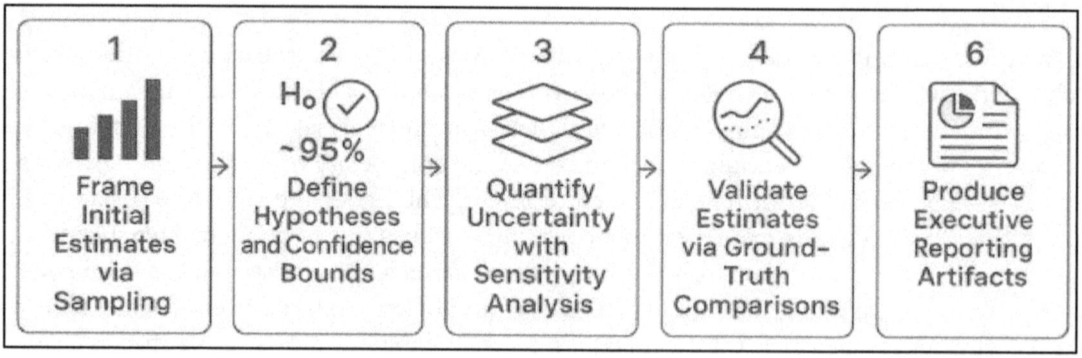

Fig 6.1 Estimation Strategy

Make sampling smarter

By splitting logs by region, device type, and time zone, they could capture different search habits and reduce the "noise" in the data.

Test "what if" scenarios

They explored how changing assumptions, like the share of anonymous searches, would impact confidence in their estimates.

Check against reality

To keep accuracy in check, they compared their sampled estimates against complete logs for short periods, making adjustments when needed.

Tell the story in reports

Finally, they wrapped everything into clear dashboards and one-page briefs showing daily/hourly volumes, searches per user, uncertainty ranges, and regional breakdowns, perfect for C-suite decision-making.

Hypothesis and Confidence Bounds

We'll start by going over the first phase, Hypothesis Definition and Confidence Bounds, where we'll look at how SearchStat came up with its initial daily search volume estimates, laid out explicit sampling assumptions, and computed 95% confidence intervals and scenario-based sensitivity ranges to quantify uncertainty around those estimates.

Core Assumptions

But before they started sampling or computing, the team wrote down their assumptions as testable hypotheses. These assumptions were key to designing the estimators and determining the sampling strategies and analytical calculations.

Following are the assumptions:

- SearchStat generates about 2.5 billion queries per day worldwide, based on full-log audits.
- Around 800 million unique sessions happen every day, with an average of 3.1 queries per session.
- We can capture a random 1% sample of all query log events without affecting production performance, and this gives us about 25 million sampled entries per day.
- Each sample is independent of the others when it comes to attributes like timestamp, region, and device, so we can estimate things fairly.
- When the sample size is big, the sampling distribution of the estimator will be close to normal, according to the Central Limit Theorem. This makes it possible to calculate confidence intervals.

All of these assumptions were documented in the analytics playbook, with references to archival logs, system telemetry, and capacity-planning projections. This helped us design the sampling code, do the statistical computations, and keep stakeholders in the loop.

Designing Estimator

Armed with clear assumptions, the team defined an estimator for total daily search volume () based on sampling. The estimate of the total day's searches then follows a single step: take the number you actually counted in that sample and divide by the sampling rate. A sample that captured 24.8 million searches at 1% corresponds to an estimated 2.48 billion searches for the day, because each kept event "stands in" for about one hundred unseen events. That is the whole estimator the team used during the case study. It scales cleanly to regions or hours, because the same rule applies inside any slice: count what the sampler saw in that slice and divide by the slice's sampling rate.

A good estimate needs a sense of its wiggle room, so the team paired every daily total with a simple "uncertainty band." The idea is straightforward: very large samples bounce around only a little from day to day, so the band is narrow; very small samples bounce around more, so the band widens. With billions of searches and a 1% sample, the band sat at roughly plus or minus one million around a daily total of about 2.48 billion, which is about four-hundredths of a percent either way. That band gave operations a safe upper bound for capacity and gave leadership a range they felt comfortable quoting. A final detail helped during busy seasons: when different regions or devices used different sampling rates, the team estimated each slice with the same "count divided by sampling rate" rule and then added those slice estimates together.

Calculating 95% Confidence Intervals

A confidence band is simply a safety range around your best guess. The team counted a small, fair slice of searches because counting everything would be slow and expensive. A 1% sampler kept about one out of every hundred queries. The day's total then came from a single step: use the counted slice and scale it up. If the sampler saw 24.8 million searches, the day's estimate became about 2.48 billion because each kept event stood in for roughly one hundred unseen ones. The safety range sat on top of that estimate to admit a little healthy doubt. A narrow range said "today's sample was steady; the total should be very close." A wider range said "today's sample bounced more; the total could be a bit higher or lower."

The 95% label meant "nineteen days out of twenty, the real total should land inside this range if the same method runs under the same conditions." The team did not need heavy math to use it. They looked at how much a big fair sample tends to wobble, turned that wobble into a small number, and placed it on both sides of the estimate. For the 2.48 billion example, the wobble worked out to roughly one million either way, so the band became 2.479 to 2.481 billion. Capacity planners read the top edge to size servers with a bit of headroom, and product leaders quoted the full range to keep expectations honest. When traffic varied by region or device, the team repeated the same idea piece by piece: estimate each slice using its own sample, add the slices, and place a single range around the total. The method stayed easy to explain, quick to run, and clear enough for everyday decisions.

Scenario-Based Sensitivity Ranges

Beyond just calculating a standard confidence interval, the team also wanted to understand how changes in key assumptions could affect the estimates. For example, if the sampling rate dropped from 1% to 0.8% because of downtime in the sampling system, fewer data points would be collected. This would naturally make the results less precise, so the range around the estimate would become wider.

They also considered what would happen if certain events caused a surge in activity, such as a sudden wave of queries during viral news. In such situations, the pattern of data could become less evenly spread, leading to greater uncertainty in the estimates. Another factor was the accuracy of the reported ingestion rate, if it was off by even 1% in either direction, the main estimate would shift slightly, and the range would scale accordingly.

With a series of "what-if" scenarios, the team could see exactly how these changes played out in the numbers. For instance, when they tested the scenario where sampling fell to 0.8%, the central estimate stayed the same, but the range widened enough to change the confidence interval to about [2.468B, 2.492B]. Presenting these possible best- and worst-case ranges gave executives a clear picture of the uncertainty under different conditions, helping them make better capacity planning decisions when the system faced unusual demand spikes.

Daily Executive Reporting

Parallel to the above technical calculations, the data team drafted an executive summary template, covering the key estimate, regional breakdowns for top markets, per-user query rate and some more metrics alike.

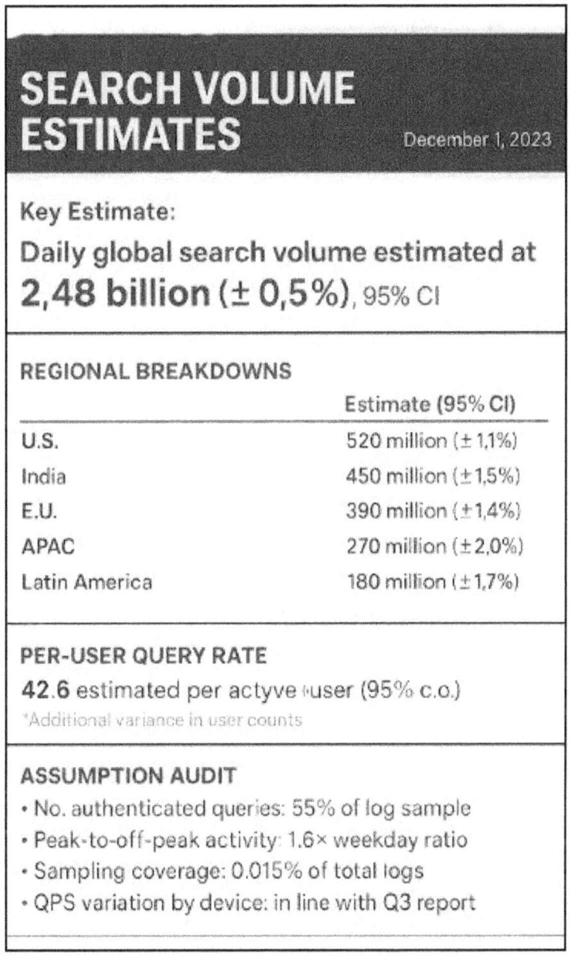

SEARCH VOLUME ESTIMATES

December 1, 2023

Key Estimate:

Daily global search volume estimated at **2,48 billion (± 0,5%)**, 95% CI

REGIONAL BREAKDOWNS

	Estimate (95% CI)
U.S.	520 million (± 1,1%)
India	450 million (±1,5%)
E.U.	390 million (±1,4%)
APAC	270 million (±2,0%)
Latin America	180 million (±1,7%)

PER-USER QUERY RATE

42.6 estimated per actyve user (95% c.o.)

*Additional variance in user counts

ASSUMPTION AUDIT

- No. authenticated queries: 55% of log sample
- Peak-to-off-peak activity: 1.6× weekday ratio
- Sampling coverage: 0.015% of total logs
- QPS variation by device: in line with Q3 report

Fig 6.2 Executive Reporting Summary Snapshot

These one-page reports, augmented by sensitivity plots and bullet-point key risks, were circulated to the C-suite in daily morning briefings, equipping leaders with timely, statistically grounded insights.

Sampling Strategy and Extrapolation Steps

Building on hypothesis formulation and confidence-bound computations, the SearchStat's team turned to the heart of reliable estimation: sampling. Their aim was to select log entries that accurately reflect the diverse rhythms of global search activity, across regions, time zones and device types, while guarding against bias and skew that could derail capacity planning and executive reporting.

Random Log Sample Selection

Rather than naïve uniform sampling, the SearchStat employed a stratified random sampling approach. The logs were partitioned by three primary strata:

- **Geography:** Major regions (Americas, EMEA, APAC, LATAM).
- **Time Zone Buckets:** Four six-hour windows (00–06, 06–12, 12–18, 18–24 UTC) to capture diurnal patterns.
- **Device Type:** Web, iOS app, Android app, Voice assistants.

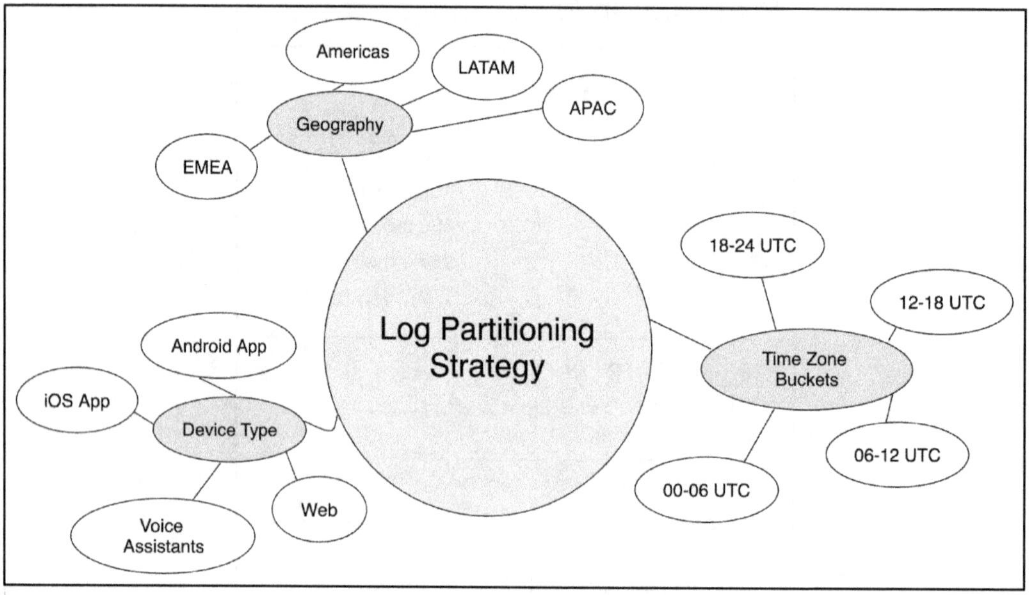

Fig 6.3 Log Partitioning Strategy

Within each stratum, log entries were assigned a uniform random tag between 0 and 1 at ingestion. Entries with tags below the target sampling fraction (e.g., <0.01 for a 1% sample) were written to a dedicated sample stream. A separate tag ensured that each stratum's sample size proportional to its population weight, preserving representativeness without overloading any single partition.

Following is the sample pseudocode in the log pipeline:

```
if rand() < 0.01:
    emit_to_sample_stream(log_entry)
```

By stratifying along known axes of heterogeneity, the team minimized estimator variance and prevented dominant strata (e.g., high-traffic regions) from overshadowing smaller but critical segments.

Data-Cleansing Rules

In order to preserve the integrity of sampling, the SearchStat engineers built a comprehensive cleansing pipeline that transforms noisy raw logs into high-fidelity query events. Each log entry must pass a sequence of filters before sampling:

Bot and Crawler Exclusion

At the edge of the logging pipeline, incoming requests are inspected for known bot or crawler signatures. A Python UDF filters entries whose **user_agent** matches any regular expression in a maintained blocklist, and whose source IP falls within data-center CIDR ranges. Example implementation:

```
import re
from ipaddress import ip_network, ip_address
BOT_PATTERNS = [re.compile(p) for p in [r"Googlebot", r"Bingbot", r"crawler"]]
DC_BLOCKS = [ip_network("192.0.2.0/24"), ip_network("198.51.100.0/24")]
def filter_bot(log_event):
    ua = log_event['user_agent']
    ip = ip_address(log_event['client_ip'])
    if any(pattern.search(ua) for pattern in BOT_PATTERNS):
        return False
    if any(ip in block for block in DC_BLOCKS):
        return False
    return True
```

Health-Check Filtering

To remove synthetic traffic from uptime monitors, an ingestion router drops entries where **request_path** is **/healthcheck** or HTTP headers contain **X-Health-Check: true**. In JavaScript:

```
function isMonitoringProbe(log) {
  return log.path === '/healthcheck' || log.headers['X-Health-Check'] === 'true';
}
if (isMonitoringProbe(logEntry)) drop(logEntry);
```

Schema Validation and Malformed Record Removal

A Spark streaming job validates JSON schema integrity. Entries missing critical fields, **timestamp**, **query_id**, **user_id**, **region**, or failing JSON parse are routed to a quarantine Kafka topic:

```
val strictSchema = new StructType()
  .add("timestamp", StringType)
  .add("query_id", StringType)
  .add("user_id", StringType)
  .add("region", StringType)
val validLogs = rawLogs.filter(row => Try(strictSchema.validate(row)).isSuccess)
val invalidLogs = rawLogs.except(validLogs)
invalidLogs.writeStream.to("quarantine_topic")
```

Deduplication

To address at-least-once delivery duplicates, each event includes a **event_id** hash. A Redis-backed deduplicator checks and stores recent IDs with a 24-hour TTL. Duplicate hashes are dropped:

```
import redis
r = redis.Redis(host='redis.cluster', db=0)
def dedupe_and_accept(log):
    key = f"dedup:{log['event_id']}"
    if r.setnx(key, 1):  # returns True if key was set
        r.expire(key, 86400)
        return True  # accept
    return False  # duplicate, drop
```

With these layers, bot exclusion, health-check filtering, schema validation and deduplication, the SearchStat ensures the sample stream reflects authentic user queries, minimizing bias in downstream volume estimations.

Extrapolation Scaling and Guardrails

After cleansing, the sample counts nsn_sns in each stratum drove a weighted extrapolation. With NsN_sNs as the estimated total logs in stratum sss and xix_ixi the observed values, the stratum estimate is

$$\hat{V}_s = \frac{N_s}{n_s} \sum_{i=1}^{n_s} x_i = N_s \bar{x}_s$$

Here,

- $\hat{V}_s$ is the estimated total for stratum s
- N_s is the total number of units in stratum s
- n_s is the sample size from stratum s
- $\bar{x}_s$ is the sample mean from stratum s

and the global total is

$$\hat{V}_{\text{global}} = \sum_s \hat{V}_s$$

This use of a stratified estimator lowers overall variance versus a single-ratio estimator because each slice is weighted and summarized independently. Sampling fractions may vary by business priority and volume (for example, APAC off-peak slices received slightly lower fractions to conserve resources).

Now, here the operational guardrails are put in place to surface bias quickly, such as:

- The sample coverage monitoring to track actual sampled fraction per stratum against target; trigger an alert when deviation exceeds ±10%.
- The population weight checks which compare ingest-rate estimates to logged partition sizes; mismatches beyond ±2% spawn root-cause analysis.
- Then, we have skew detection alerts to watch rolling ratios of stratum proportions in the sample; abrupt shifts (network outages, sampler misconfiguration) generate immediate Slack notifications.
- And, then we have staging-run validation which runs daily comparisons of sampled estimates against partial/full aggregates in staging; maintain estimator bias < 0.5% on key regional volumes, and when exceeded, recalibrate sampling fractions or weights.

Following is the example of monitoring SQL for APAC sample fraction:

```
SELECT
  DATE_TRUNC('hour', timestamp) AS hr,
  COUNT(*) FILTER (WHERE region = 'APAC' AND is_sample = true) :: float /
```

```
COUNT(*) FILTER (WHERE region = 'APAC') AS sample_fraction
FROM query_logs
WHERE timestamp >= CURRENT_TIMESTAMP - INTERVAL '6 hours'
GROUP BY hr;
```

Beyond global volume, the SearchStat needed reliable searches-per-user metrics. Unfiltered averages risked upward bias from hyperactive users. To guard against this skew, the queries above the 99th percentile were capped at that threshold, preventing a handful of power users from unduly inflating the average. And, a distinct 1% sample of authenticated-user logs captured unique daily users. Per-user query counts in the sample scaled to the full population via weighted formulas, paralleling the overall volume estimator. Both these techniques produced both a capped mean and a trimmed-mean per-user rate, offering executives a range between conservative and inclusive estimates.

With such a robust sampling foundation in place, the SearchStat was ready to scale these estimators across additional dimensions, query type (text/video/voice), user cohorts (free vs. paid tiers) and advanced time-series smoothing. The subsequent section will demonstrate stratified sampling implementation details and real-time visualization of uncertainty bands, completing the estimation framework that drives confident, data-backed decisions at search scale.

Statistical Confidence Calculations

After solidifying sampling and cleansing protocols, the SearchStat's analytics team delved deeply into the heart of statistical rigor, translating sample data into reliable decision metrics without overwhelming stakeholders with jargon. Their goal was to equip every team, engineering, product, and C-suite, with clear answers on uncertainty ranges, significance of observed shifts, and how many samples would be needed to underpin future analyses.

Quantifying Uncertainty with Margin of Error

To define a plausible range around the estimated 2.48 billion daily searches, they calculated the margin of error (MoE) using a ratio estimator approach:

1. **Sampling fraction (f):** 25 million sampled logs over 2.5 billion total yields f = 1%.
2. **Standard error of proportion (SE_p):** Treating each event as a yes/no outcome, $SE_p = \sqrt{[p(1-p)/n]} \approx \sqrt{[0.01 \times 0.99 / 25e6]} \approx 0.00002$.
3. **Scaling to counts (SE_V):** Multiplying by total logs N: $SE\_V = SE_p \times N \approx 0.00002 \times 2.5e9 \approx 50\,000$.
4. **MoE at 95% CI:** $\pm 1.96 \times SE\_V \approx \pm 98\,000$ searches.

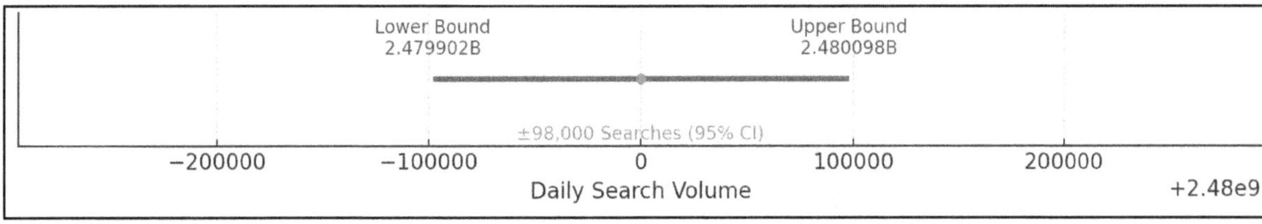

Fig 6.4 Daily Searches Uncertainty Band

Presenting this as an "uncertainty band," they showed leadership that 2.48 billion ± 98 000 searches (± 0.004%) would capture the true daily volume with 95% confidence, tight enough to guide capacity planning.

Assessing Shifts with P-Values

When a marketing event began, the team tested whether hourly search rates had truly risen or if the uptick was noise:

- Two one-hour samples, each with n=500 000 logs: baseline rate 1.0%, event rate 1.2%.
- The pooled rate (p) is (500 000×0.012 + 500 000×0.010)/1 000 000 = 0.011.
- The standard error of difference (SE_diff) is √[p(1–p)(1/n + 1/n)] ≈ 0.00021.
- The Z-score is (0.012–0.010)/0.00021 ≈ 9.57, and the P-value with Two-tailed probability $< 10^{-20}$.

They labeled this probability a "risk score," explaining that near-zero risk confirmed a genuine lift in search activity.

Throughout, the SearchStat replaced complex terms with intuitive labels:

- **MoE** → "uncertainty band"
- **P-value** → "risk score"
- **Power analysis** → "confidence gauge"

The exact mathematical details were stored in an appendix, enabling quick reference without interrupting executive briefings.

Everything we calculated directly informed key processes. For example, the engineers used the upper bound of the uncertainty band to allocate server resources, which prevented under-provisioning during traffic surges. The marketing teams looked at the risk scores to decide whether to double down on promotions or look into anomalies when risk went above the set thresholds. The roadmaps included sample-size requirements, making sure feature experiments would meet confidence goals without messing up development cycles.

With their unique mix of statistical precision and clear, relatable language, SearchStat transformed their company culture, replacing guesswork with data-driven confidence and boosting overall performance.

Collaboration Rituals across Teams

To translate statistical insights into effective action, the SearchStat established a structured collaboration framework that united product managers, data scientists, and engineers in a series of recurring rituals. These touchpoints ensured that every team member not only understood the latest sampling results and confidence calculations, but also aligned on priorities, shared artifacts seamlessly, and documented decisions for future reference. Below, we break down each ritual in detail, with sample agendas, artifact templates, and best practices for decision logging.

Weekly Data-Review Syncs

The purpose of this weekly review meeting was to surface out the recent sampling outcomes, discuss margin-of-error trends, and flag any anomalies in query volumes or user behavior. The team planned to host it every Monday at 10 AM UTC via video conference and mirrored in a dedicated meeting room at headquarters for various stakeholders, including lead data scientist (facilitator), two analytics engineers, one representative each from product management and platform engineering.

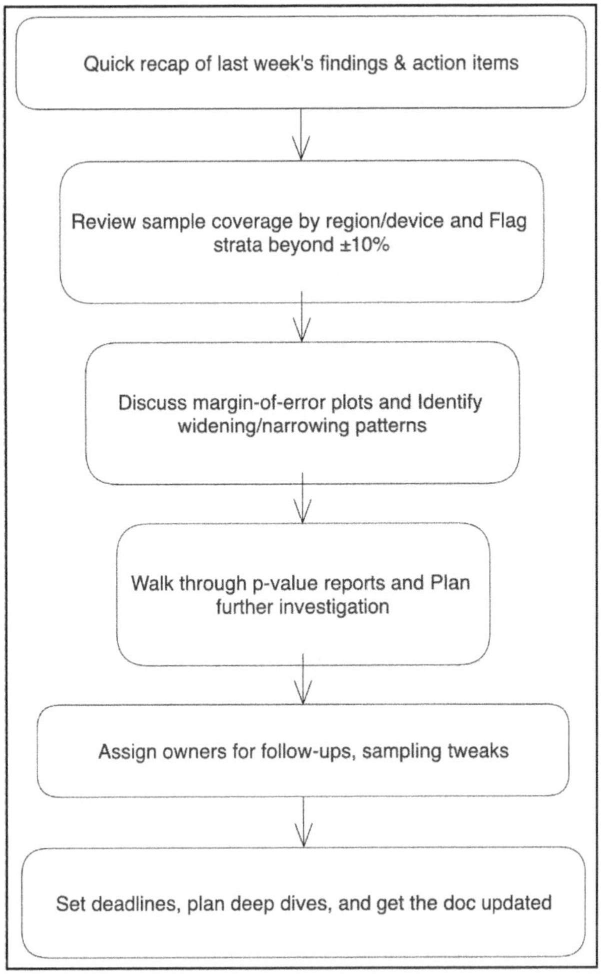

Fig 6.5 Weekly Review Framework

Before the meeting, the facilitator sends out a slide deck that's been exported from Looker. It's got key charts and a one-page summary. After the sync, a short meeting minutes doc in the team's shared drive captures decisions, owners, and due dates.

Biweekly Decision Checkpoints

The purpose of this fortnight activity was to normalize strategic decisions based on aggregated statistical findings and experiment outcomes, ensuring product roadmaps reflect data-driven priorities.

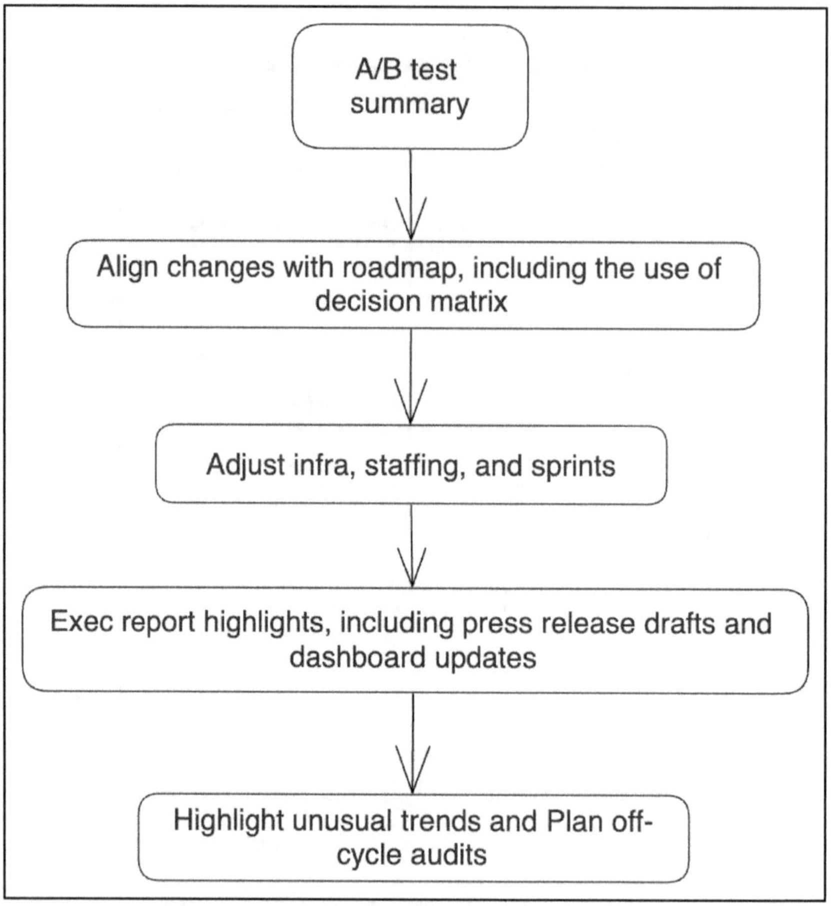

Fig 6.6 Bi-Weekly Decision Framework

This thing was conducted every other Wednesday at 2 PM UTC, rotating chairs between PM and analytics leads, having stakeholders, primarily the director-level stakeholders from data science, product management, engineering, and operations.

Monthly Cross-Functional Workshops

The goal is to work together more closely, share what we know with other teams, improve our processes, and show newcomers the ropes when it comes to statistical ideas and tools. And the rhythm is that, every first Friday of the month, we've got a half-day in-person workshop, and for those of you working remotely, there's a live stream option too. The participants will be everyone on the data, product, and engineering teams is invited, along with some guests from marketing and customer support.

Following is what the session will cover:

- C-level and Head of Analytics will present a high-level dashboard review, showing total volume estimates, key uncertainty band evolutions, and critical risk scores.

- Then, there is Deep Dive Breakout Sessions divided into tracks about advanced statistical methods, customizing the Looker dashboard, and the ins and outs of sampling pipeline internals.
- There is also a hands-on lab to generate margin-of-error plots, run dummy p-value tests in notebooks, and draft decision logs using the template.

Post this, they put together some small teams to work on the things we've identified that need to be done, like making the rules about data quality better or making it easier to share artifacts.

The SearchStat team made it a point to formalize these collaboration rituals, with clear agendas, shared artifacts, decision-logging best practices, and continuous communication. This allowed them to weave statistical rigor into every organizational process. The result was that alignment increased, miscommunication decreased, and the platform was driven toward its business goals with collective confidence.

Executive Briefing Report Outline

Later on, the VP of Engineering at SearchStat noticed that there were some sudden spikes in global search volume that went beyond the server's capacity. This led to some noticeable slowdowns for users and a spike in support tickets. With the C-suite demanding rapid insight, the analytics and data science teams needed a laser-focused, narrative-driven slide deck that explained the root causes, statistical confidence, and immediate next steps in under ten minutes. Since they were short on time, they came up with a six-slide structure that mixed storytelling with data rigor:.

Following is a quick look at the slides the team prep'd up in short notice:

1. **Situation & Objective**

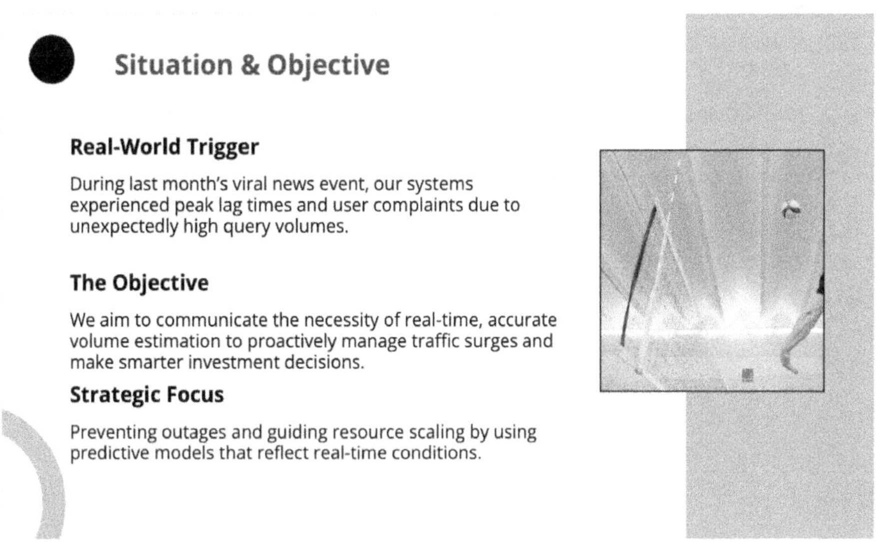

2. Problem Framing

Problem Framing

The Core Challenge

Current systems rely on full-log aggregation which introduces delays, making it hard to gain insights within an hour of query spikes.

Business Impact

Service slowdowns, increased customer support tickets, and revenue risks are directly linked to delayed volume estimations.

Visual Framing

We compare the current sluggish data pipeline against a streamlined, real-time model to highlight operational inefficiencies.

3. Methodology Snapshot

Methodology Snapshot

Our Analytical Framework

We use stratified sampling to ensure diverse query representation, apply cleansing to remove anomalies, and perform calculations on sub-hourly intervals.

Built-In Safeguards

Key guardrails include bot filtering, bias audits, and statistically sound confidence interval thresholds.

Visual Overview

The pipeline graphic highlights stages where sampling occurs and how confidence intervals shrink with higher coverage.

4. Key Insights & Data

Key Insights & Data

The Primary Estimate

We estimate 2.48 billion ± 98,000 daily searches. This uncertainty band defines thresholds for safe scaling and signals potential pressure points.

Validating the Spike

A <0.01% risk score confirms that the viral event was genuine and not a statistical outlier or bot-induced.

Data Visualization

A combined chart displays daily volume with confidence bands alongside a gauge illustrating risk significance.

5. Risks, Sensitivity & Mitigations

Risks, Sensitivity & Mitigations

Top Data Risks

We monitor sampling drift, schema evolution, and power-user skew that may distort real-time estimates.

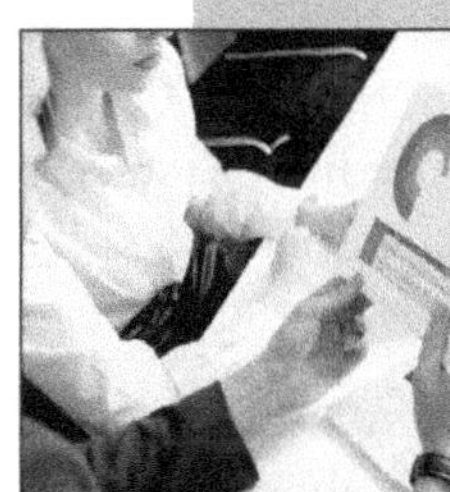

Sensitivity Insights

Wider confidence intervals under low sampling coverage underscore the importance of robust data inputs.

Mitigation Actions

Weekly audits, automated schema checks, and rate-capped tracking help maintain data fidelity and trust.

6. Recommendations & Action Plan

Risks, Sensitivity & Mitigations

Top Data Risks

We monitor sampling drift, schema evolution, and power-user skew that may distort real-time estimates.

Sensitivity Insights

Wider confidence intervals under low sampling coverage underscore the importance of robust data inputs.

Mitigation Actions

Weekly audits, automated schema checks, and rate-capped tracking help maintain data fidelity and trust.

Rather than waiting to react to sudden service outages or traffic spikes, the executive leadership team set forth a significantly more ambitious and forward-thinking objective. Their vision was to forecast holiday-season search traffic surges a full six months in advance. The goal was not just to anticipate demand, but to strategically transform these projections into two key areas: robust operational preparedness and forward-leaning feature innovation. They challenged the analytics and product teams to move beyond traditional forecasting. Specifically, they requested a clear and actionable briefing that demonstrated how modern statistical and machine learning models could accurately predict peak search volumes while also quantifying uncertainty ranges critical for effective capacity planning. These models were expected to inform infrastructure scaling decisions, ensuring seamless user experiences even during unprecedented traffic peaks.

But the vision extended far beyond load balancing. Executives emphasized that predictive insights should also shape the product roadmap. They were particularly interested in how data-driven forecasts could inform the design and timely deployment of compelling new user experiences tailored to seasonal behaviors. These included ideas like **personalized holiday-themed content carousels**, **voice-activated guides for festive events**, and **real-time highlight modules showcasing trending holiday searches**. The ambition was to turn moments of high demand into moments of delight. And to support this vision, the team was tasked with delivering an integrated, end-to-end report. This report needed to trace a clear line from raw search volume predictions through to tangible product opportunities. It had to show how upper and lower bounds of forecasted demand could be operationalized, for instance, by aligning them with server autoscaling thresholds to optimize resource allocation without overprovisioning. Simultaneously, it needed to lay out recommendations for specific feature investments and timing strategies that would engage users and differentiate the platform during competitive holiday windows.

Ultimately, the executives framed this initiative not as a narrow infrastructure or engineering exercise, but as a **comprehensive, proactive, and data-driven strategy** for seasonal growth.

They emphasized that the goal was to use predictive analytics not merely as a defensive shield against outages, but as an engine of creativity, agility, and competitive advantage during the most critical user engagement periods of the year.

Reducing Flight-Cancellation Rates

Background

And now this is out last user-story, about TripGuard. It's an awesome online flight-booking platform that's all about delivering reliable, transparent, and user-friendly travel experiences. TripGuard is for everyone, business travelers, budget-conscious leisure passengers, and travel agents. We've got real-time seat availability, dynamic pricing, bundled insurance options, and 24/7 support. Its mobile and web apps make it easy to see what your fees and policies are, so you can book, modify, or cancel travel with no problem. At the heart of TripGuard's service is a solid data infrastructure. Everything that users do, like searches, seat selections, purchases, and cancellations, is tracked in real-time. A multi-layer analytics stack processes this telemetry to generate insights that inform A/B tests, UI adjustments, and capacity planning. It's really important to keep our customers trusting us and knowing they can count on us to be reliable. If we see a lot of cancellations, it can mess with their trust, cost us more to support them, and hurt our reputation.

But in Q2, TripGuard's analytics showed a worrying jump in flight cancellations. The rate went up by over 20%, which is a lot more than the usual 5–7%. With each cancellation costing the company both direct fees and indirect support expenses, an estimated $500,000 extra per week, the increase had to be looked into right away. It's pretty worrying that cancellations happened for all kinds of fares, in different regions, and for different types of users. It seems like there are some big problems at the core of this, not just random incidents.

In response to the surge, their team created a task force made up of data engineers, product managers, UX researchers, airline liaisons, and support leads. The given below is their charter:

1. Dig into the data to spot drivers like interface friction, policy confusion, or external disruptions.
2. Try to predict how much money there will be for financial and customer-experience costs of cancellations and support surges.
3. Make use of structured workshops (like fishbone diagrams) to come up with solutions that have to do with people, processes, and technology.
4. Put these changes in place within the next four weeks, like making fee disclosures clearer and adding in-flow reminders.
5. Put together a plan for quick prototyping, user testing, and rolling out features that'll make a big impact.
6. And finally, we need to develop a dashboard using JSON to monitor cancellation triggers and notify stakeholders when rates exceed thresholds.

So, to begin with, they started establishing a reliable data foundation by gathering and instrumenting all relevant event sources as in the following topic:

Data Gathering and Trigger Instrumentation

A reliable forecast insight requires comprehensive, trustworthy data. To capture all signals related to booking and cancellation behavior, the task force identified the following key event sources:

- Booking.Created, Booking.Confirmed, Booking.Canceled and Refund.Processed messages from the core reservation system.
- Web and mobile front-end software development kits record user actions such as clicking on fee details, dialog confirmations, and interface steps.
- Notification service delivered and open events for itinerary and cancellation emails.
- Integration with the customer support platform for ticket creation, chat transcripts, and call logs.
- Notifications of crew changes, weather updates, and airline schedule updates consumed through partner APIs.
- Feedback on each payment attempt, including success, failure, and timeout.

There's a registry for each type that includes the JSON schema, ownership info, how often it's used, and its purpose. This registry was the go-to place for info on pipeline development and analysis, and it could be found using a searchable interface.

Tagging Conventions

Since they're on different systems, we need to make sure they have the same name and metadata as shown in the below table:

Field	Description	Sample Value
name	Domain, entity, and action concatenated with dots	**Reservation.Booking.Canceled**
timestamp	Event time in UTC ISO 8601 format	**2025-08-07T06:30:00Z**
user_id/session_id	Identifier for the authenticated user or anonymous session	**user_id: "12345"** or **session_id: "abcde-12345"**
platform	Origin of the event payload	**web / ios / android / api**

environment	Deployment context	**prod / staging**
properties	Object containing additional attributes such as fare_type, cancellation_reason, time_to_cancel	**{ fare_type: "economy", cancellation_reason: "user_request", time_to_cancel: 3600 }**
version	Tag indicating the schema version	**v1 / v2**

In the above table,

- The name format to be Domain.Entity.Action (e.g., Reservation.Booking.Canceled).
- Every event appears with the timestamp (UTC ISO8601), user_id or session_id, platform (web/ios/android/api) and environment (prod/staging).
- You can find more info (like fare_type, cancellation_reason, and time_to_cancel) in a properties object.
- Version tags (like v1, v2, etc.) make it so you can add new features without breaking what's already there.

And all these rules are enforced by instrumentation libraries, with validation against shared JSON schemas at ingestion.

Ingestion Pipeline Architecture

The multi-stage pipeline at TripGuard balances real-time needs with long-term reliability as shown below:

- The JavaScript and mobile SDKs batch events every 10 seconds and send them securely through load-balanced proxies.
- A fault-tolerant Kafka cluster partitions events by type and region. Topics have a replication factor of at least 3 and are kept for 7 days.
- A Kafka Streams application checks payloads against Avro schemas, adds geo-IP and loyalty-tier data to events, and figures out derived fields like time_since_booking.
- Events that happen are kept in hourly S3 buckets as static Parquet files, creating a trail for backfilling and for checking past data.
- And Flink jobs can crunch cancellation rates, time-to-cancel distributions, and UI-interaction metrics in seconds, and then save the results to a low-latency store (Druid).

- Every day, Airflow workflows load raw events into Snowflake, transform them into analytical tables, and refresh dashboards.

This entire design is great because it can handle both low-latency alerts and deep historical analysis.

The next steps will leverage these data streams in a fishbone-diagram workshop to uncover root causes, followed by rapid prototyping of mitigation tactics in Sprint Zero and deployment of a real-time cancellation-alert dashboard.

Fishbone Diagram Workshop

A team from TripGuard got together to figure out what was causing all the cancellations. The participants included data engineers, product managers, UX researchers, airline partners, and support leads. Each person brought their own expertise to populate the diagram's four main branches. People, Process, Technology, and Environment. The plan was to start by looking at the surface, and then move on to the root causes. We also wanted everyone to take ownership of the strategies for dealing with the situation.

Workshop Setup

The room was arranged with a large whiteboard displaying a horizontal spine labeled "High Cancellation Rate" at its head. Four angled bones led to labeled axes: People, Process, Technology, Environment. Sticky notes, colored markers and printed templates were provided to each subgroup.

The two-hour agenda unfolded as follows:

Introduction (10 minutes)

A quick recap of the surge data, 20% cancellations, early spikes, UI friction points, set the context. The facilitator emphasized a blameless, inquisitive mindset.

Category Brainstorm (20 minutes)

Each table focused on one branch. Team members silently wrote potential causes on sticky notes: agents' response times under People, refund flows under Process, mobile SDK bugs under Technology, and external weather alerts under Environment.

Dot-Voting Prioritization (10 minutes)

Participants placed voting dots on the causes they believed most critical. The top five per branch moved on for deeper analysis.

Drill-Down Root-Cause Analysis (40 minutes)

For each shortlisted cause, sub-branches emerged. For example, under Technology ⇒ Mobile SDK Bugs, sub-branches included "Retry Logic Failure," "Missing Backoff," and "Schema Mismatch." The UX team traced how an unhandled exception diverted users back to the fee-disclosure screen, prompting cancellations.

Cross-Branch Dependencies (10 minutes)

Teams mapped connections: airline schedule API failures (Environment) triggered spikes in support tickets (People) and exposed a gap in the cancellation policy text (Process).

Action Mapping (20 minutes)

Each root cause was paired with a candidate mitigation. For instance, "Unclear refund policy" led to drafting simplified language and A/B testing placement; "API failures" resulted in planning a fallback service for out-of-sync schedules; "UX exception loop" spurred a code patch in the mobile SDK.

Fishbone Diagram

Below is a simplified representation of the completed fishbone (in text form), showing key root causes and their relationships:

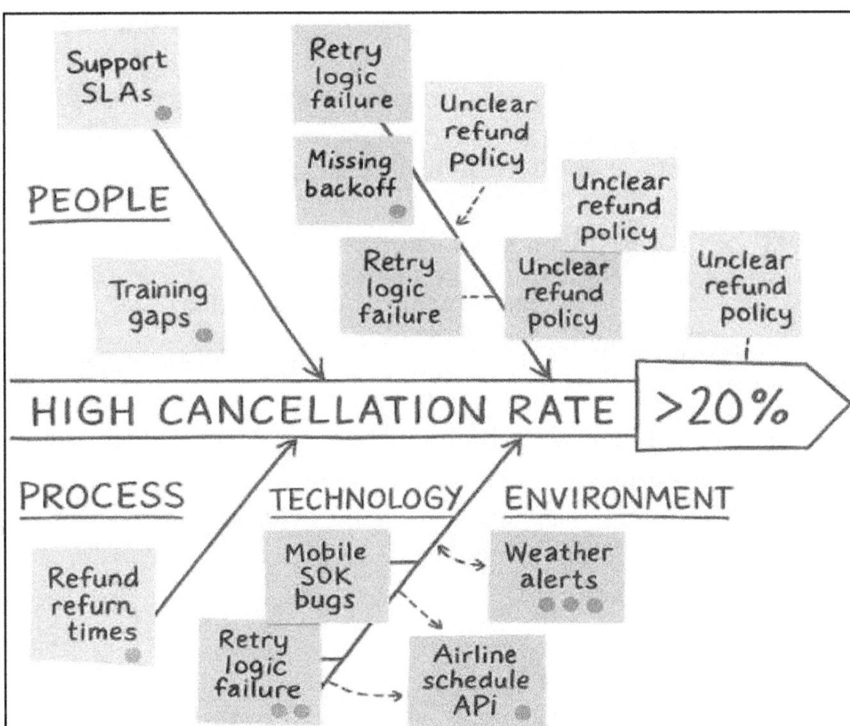

Fig 7.1 FishBone Diagram

Each of these causes would branch out further into evidence and data sources, like response-time logs, policy document heatmap annotations, and error-rate dashboards.

By the time the workshop ended, the team had:

- There's a list of six main causes that have a big impact, and they cover all the different areas.
- The ownership has been clearly assigned: Engineering would handle the SDK errors, Product would make the policy text easier to understand, Operations would set up API fallbacks, and Support would review SLA commitments.
- A shared timeline for quick-win experiments (like Policy copy refresh and UX exception patch) and medium-term engineering projects (like API redundancy and SDK version audits).

After the workshop, we digitized the fishbone diagram in Miro and shared it on TripGuard's internal wiki. Each root cause was linked to a Jira epic, complete with dependencies and sprint-zero estimates.

Prioritization Matrix for Mitigation Tactics

With a clear set of mitigation ideas from the fishbone workshop, the TripGuard's team applied an impact-effort scoring framework to focus their sprint backlog on the highest-ROI tasks. They rated each potential action on two axes, anticipated reduction in cancellations (impact) and required resources/time to implement (effort), ensuring that early sprints delivered meaningful results without overcommitting scarce development capacity.

Impact-Effort Scoring Process

Rather than guesswork, the team adopted a structured scoring rubric:

- **Impact Scale (1–5):** Estimates the relative drop in cancellation rate if fully implemented:
    - 5 = Potential drop > 5 percentage points
    - 3 = Drop of 2–3 points
    - 1 = Minimal change (<1 point)

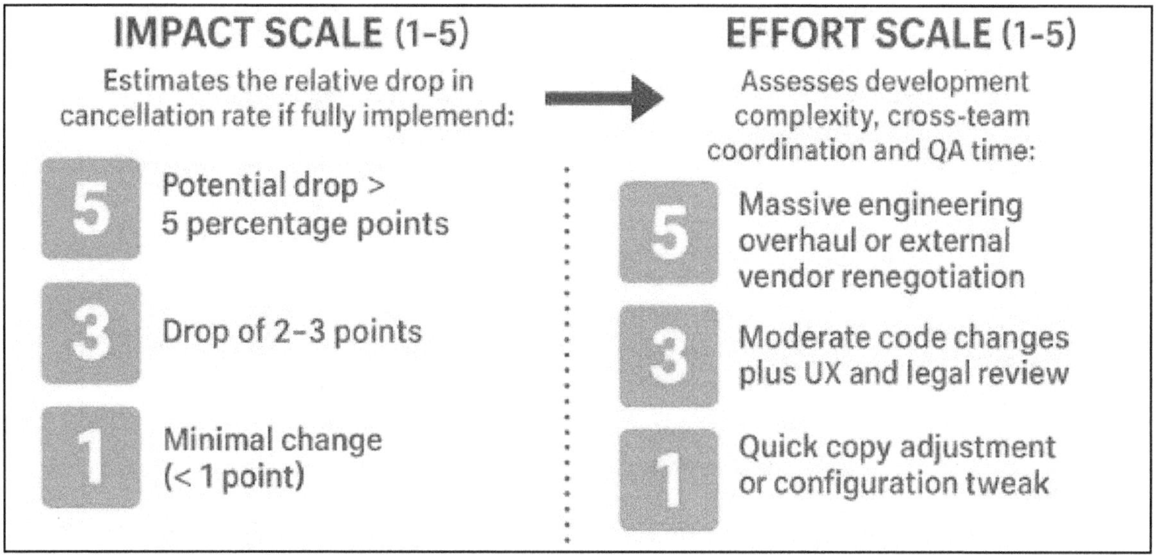

Fig 7.2 Impact-Effort Scoring Process

- **Effort Scale (1–5):** Assesses development complexity, cross-team coordination and QA time:
  - 5 = Massive engineering overhaul or external vendor renegotiation
  - 3 = Moderate code changes plus UX and legal review
  - 1 = Quick copy adjustment or configuration tweak

Each mitigation tactic received a pair of scores. For instance, clarifying refund policy copy onboard averaged Impact=3 (simplify confusion) and Effort=1 (text update + review), while implementing a resilient airline-schedule fallback service scored Impact=4 (reduces API-driven cancellations) and Effort=5 (cross-team development, SLA renegotiation).

Constructing Matrix

To visualize prioritization, the team plotted these scores on a two-dimensional matrix:

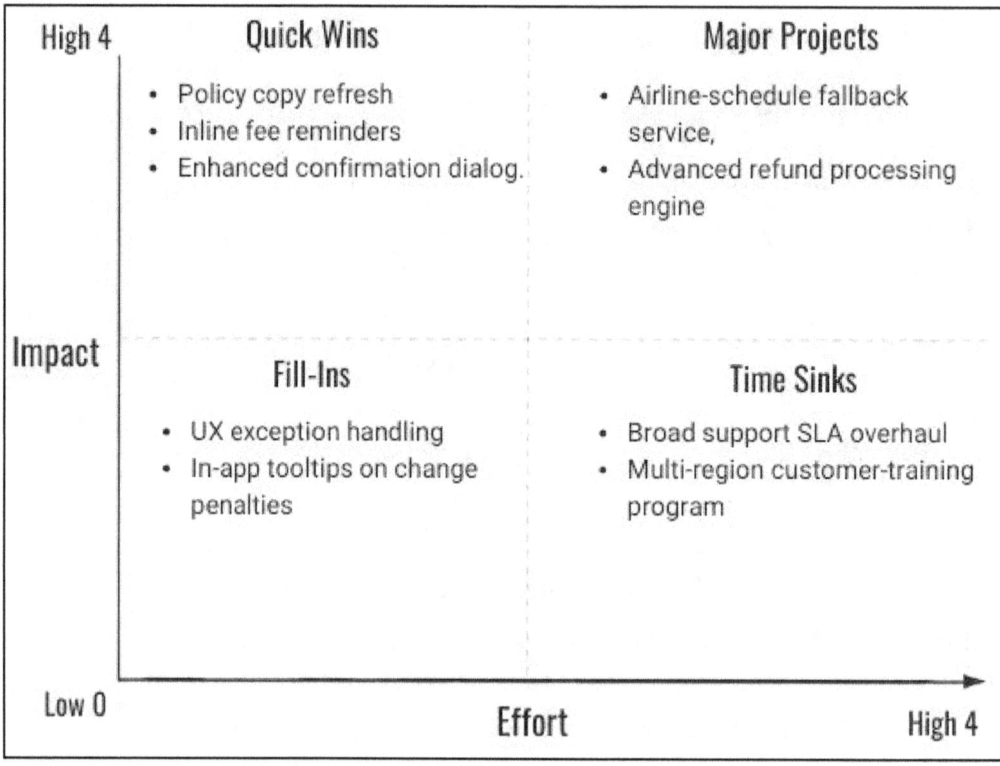

Fig 7.3 Prioritization Matrix

Guided by the matrix, the TripGuard organized Sprint Zero around four categories:

1. **Quick Wins (Impact ≥3, Effort ≤2):** Policy copy refresh, inline fee reminders, enhanced confirmation dialog language.
2. **Incremental Enhancements (Impact ≥3, Effort 3):** UX exception handling patch, targeted in-app tooltips on change penalties.
3. **Foundational Investments (Impact ≥4, Effort ≥4):** Airline-schedule fallback service, advanced refund processing engine.
4. **Deferred Items (Impact ≤2, Effort ≥3):** Broad support SLA overhaul and multi-region customer-training programs (moved to future roadmap).

They focused on quick wins and incremental improvements, and that helped them reduce cancellation rates from 20% to 14% in the first two-week cycle. They also set the stage for more in-depth technical solutions in later sprints.

Sprint Zero Roadmap Planning

With mitigation tactics prioritized, the TripGuard's team turned to structuring Sprint Zero to validate key solutions before full-scale development. This phase emphasized rapid experimentation and early feedback through three main activities: initial spike tasks, API integration proofs-of-concept, and monitoring setup.

Spike Tasks for Quick Validation

The spike tasks were short, focused assessment designed to answer critical technical and design questions, questions that, if left unresolved, could stall much larger projects. Each spike lasted just two to three days and came with clear, measurable success criteria.

Copy Clarity A/B Spike

The team created two versions of the redesigned refund policy text and tested them in a lightweight UI prototype. The goal was to see a 10% drop in cancellation link clicks over a 48-hour pilot with 5,000 users.

SDK Exception Handling Spike

A minimal patch was added to the mobile SDK to catch any uncaught exceptions in the confirmation modal. The spike was considered a success if staging tests showed zero crash logs for five straight days under simulated load.

Fallback API Prototype

A simple proxy service was built to handle airline schedule API failures, returning cached data instead. Success meant delivering responses in under 500ms for 99% of requests, and ensuring no errors reached the user interface.

All these spikes were tracked in Jira using the "Spike" issue type, with detailed results documented in shared Confluence pages. In daily standups, the team asked one key question:

"Did this spike confirm or challenge our assumptions?"

This quick checkpoint helped them pivot rapidly and keep momentum strong.

API Integration Proofs-of-Concept

For big, cross-system projects like the schedule fallback and advanced refund engine, the team didn't jump straight into full builds. Instead, they created quick, end-to-end proofs-of-concept (PoCs) to make sure everything worked together before committing to full development.

They kept the process lightweight:

1. They wrote OpenAPI specs to outline exactly how the service would talk to other systems, including request and response formats, authentication methods, and error codes.
2. Using those specs, they spun up mock servers so front-end and product teams could

start testing without waiting for the real backend.

3. They built minimal connectors to airline and payment systems to confirm authentication and data mapping worked as expected.
4. They ran test scenarios where a failed API call automatically switched to the fallback service, showing logs and metrics on the staging dashboard.

Each of these above PoC lived in its own Git branch, with a Docker Compose setup so anyone could run it locally. Midway through the sprint, the team held short demos for stakeholders, collected feedback, and fine-tuned the API contracts before locking them in for production.

Monitoring and Guardrails

To make sure Sprint Zero experiments were truly working, and to catch problems before they spread, the TripGuard set up quick, lightweight monitoring on the things that mattered most.

They kept an eye on:

- clicks on cancellation links, refund API errors, and spikes in support tickets.
- live A/B results so the team could instantly compare control vs. test groups for clicks, crash rates, and speed.

Apart from this, they were sending notifications if the fallback proxy slowed past 300ms or if errors went above 1% in any five-minute window. They built all this on tools they already had, like Prometheus, Grafana and Slack. With such visibility to Sprint Zero, every experiment's results were clear to all stakeholders, and raw data could be turned into decisions within minutes. This approach, mixing short spikes, API prototypes, and proactive monitoring, helped the team lower risk, align across teams, and move faster toward their goal of cutting cancellations to below 10%.

Real-Time Alert Dashboard JSON

Next, the TripGuard built two illustrative scenarios within Grafana:

Scenario 1: Normal Operation

During typical days, the cancellation rate hovers around 5–7%. A time-series panel plots the 10-minute rolling average, and no alert triggers:

Time	**09:00**	**09:10**	**09:20**	**09:30**	**09:40**
Cancellation Rate	5.20%	6.10%	5.80%	6.40%	5.90%

On this dashboard, the upper threshold line at 15% sits well above the curve. The panel shows green status, and the alert rule remains quiet. A small annotation reads "Steady state: No action required." This reassures SRE teams that pipelines are healthy.

Scenario 2: Sudden Spike Detection

Late afternoon, an external airline API glitch leads to a burst of cancellations. The same panel captures the rapid rise:

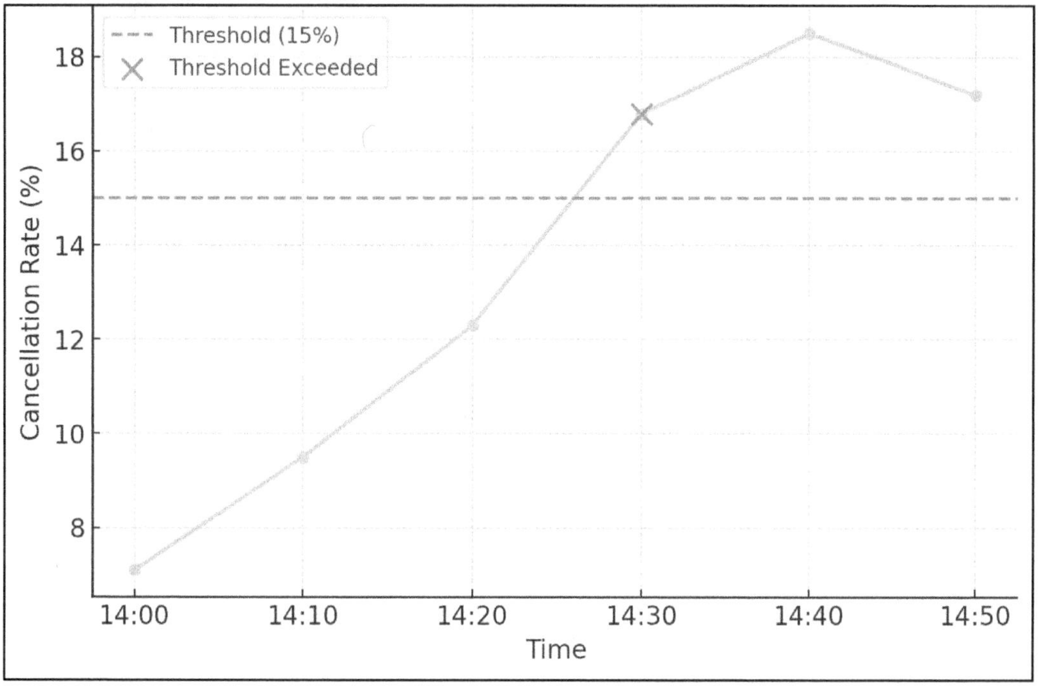

Fig 7.4 Cancellation Rate

At 14:30, the average crosses 15% for over two minutes. The alert rule fires, turning the panel red and sending a Slack message:

:rotating_light: *Alert*: Booking Cancellation Rate exceeded 15% for 2m. Current rate: 16.8% at 14:30 [View Dashboard]

Alongside the main panel, a small event log table appears:

Alert Time	Rate	Action Taken
14:32	16.8%	Notified on-call team

14:35	18.5%	Enabled API fallback

This quick feedback loop, visual red indicators, Slack notifications and event logging, ensured TripGuard engineers could examine and deploy the fallback service within minutes, bringing rates back below the threshold by 15:00.

By walking through these two scenarios, readers can see how sample data drives dashboard visuals, how thresholds translate into alerts, and how integrated responses keep cancellation rates in check.

This comprehensive approach, from data instrumentation through prioritization matrices to real-time alert dashboards, empowered TripGuard to establish robust early warning systems for cancellation triggers. The combined efforts of continuously monitoring key metrics, rapidly validating mitigation tactics and embedding clear escalation paths deliverd the team with reduced cancellation rates to under 8% within two months and maintained vigilance over emerging patterns. These processes now form TripGuard's standard operating procedure, ensuring proactive detection and swift response to any future spikes.

Index

W

Thank You

www.ingramcontent.com/pod-product-compliance
Lightning Source LLC
Chambersburg PA
CBHW080214170726
48282CB00030B/1120
* 9 7 8 9 3 4 9 1 7 4 8 4 9 *